Just Spring Integration

Madhusudhan Konda

O'REILLY®

Beijing · Cambridge · Farnham · Köln · Sebastopol · Tokyo

Just Spring Integration
by Madhusudhan Konda

Copyright © 2012 Madhusudhan Konda. All rights reserved.
Printed in the United States of America.

Published by O'Reilly Media, Inc., 1005 Gravenstein Highway North, Sebastopol, CA 95472.

O'Reilly books may be purchased for educational, business, or sales promotional use. Online editions are also available for most titles (*http://my.safaribooksonline.com*). For more information, contact our corporate/institutional sales department: (800) 998-9938 or *corporate@oreilly.com*.

Editors:	Mike Loukides and Meghan Blanchette	**Cover Designer:**	Karen Montgomery
Production Editor:	Rachel Steely	**Interior Designer:**	David Futato
Copyeditor:	Chet Chin	**Illustrators:**	Robert Romano and Rebecca Demarest
Proofreader:	Rachel Steely		

Revision History for the First Edition:
    2012-03-30   First release
See *http://oreilly.com/catalog/errata.csp?isbn=9781449316082* for release details.

ISBN: 978-1-449-31608-2

[LSI]

1333127284

Table of Contents

Foreword

It's a tough challenge to find the right depth and the right level of abstraction when introducing a new technology. A book can go too deep, and risk miring the reader in technological minutiae. This is hardly helpful, and—more often than not—it's boring. A book can also stay at a very abstract level, and revel in theory, but even this is boring and useless for someone who hopes to achieve anything useful. Instead, the best books treat a new technology as a dark room. They hold your hand and introduce the concepts as you're likely to encounter them, while saving you from missteps that you might otherwise make. This is one such book: it introduces the concepts of Spring Integration's API, along with their designs, but lets you move onto the next subject and keep the entire mental map of the room in your head.

If you're new to integration, and new to Spring Integration in particular, then let Madhusudhan Konda hold your hand and lead you to the light ahead, in this easy-to-read guide, *Just Spring Integration*. When you're done, you'll be up and running, and if you still need more details, then you can always consult the Spring Integration project page (*http://www.springsource.org/spring-integration*) for in-depth features and access to the forums.

—Josh Long

Preface

Messaging is a complex creature.

When I first started working on Enterprise projects in early 2000, I was initially lost in the jungles of Enterprise messaging. It was (and is still, to some extent) a formidable challenge to start an Enterprise messaging project. There used to be a variety of messaging product offerings in the market, each one capable of performing several functions. The JMS and JCA specs were handy, although a bit dry and hard to grasp without a substantial amount of time spent on understanding them.

Projects do exist in an environment where it is necessary to interact and integrate with other systems or modules. Integrating with other systems is a challenge to any Enterprise developer. I have worked with many developers who really wish to have a good grasp of messaging frameworks but have been discouraged by the complexities and technological offerings. I always wondered if there were an integration framework that could take away the hassle of working with disparate systems.

Then came the Spring Integration framework. The Spring team has gone the extra mile to simplify the complexities around messaging by creating the Integration framework, complete with all sorts of bells and whistles. Spring Integration Framework is a perfect fit for any Enterprise or standalone messaging application.

This book is an attempt to demystify the framework. It should give you enough knowledge and confidence to start working on real world projects.

My aim is to deliver a simple, straightforward, no-nonsense, and example-driven book on Spring Integration Framework. Of course, I'd like it to be a page turner and easy to read, as well. I hope that I have achieved that through this book.

Please do get in touch should you have any feedback on this book. I hope you will enjoy *Just Spring Integration* as much as I enjoyed writing it.

Conventions Used in This Book

The following typographical conventions are used in this book:

Italic

Indicates new terms, URLs, email addresses, filenames, and file extensions.

`Constant width`

Used for program listings, as well as within paragraphs to refer to program elements such as variable or function names, databases, data types, environment variables, statements, and keywords.

`Constant width bold`

Shows commands or other text that should be typed literally by the user.

`Constant width italic`

Shows text that should be replaced with user-supplied values or by values determined by context.

 This icon signifies a tip, suggestion, or general note.

 This icon indicates a warning or caution.

Using Code Examples

This book is here to help you get your job done. In general, you may use the code in this book in your programs and documentation. You do not need to contact us for permission unless you're reproducing a significant portion of the code. For example, writing a program that uses several chunks of code from this book does not require permission. Selling or distributing a CD-ROM of examples from O'Reilly books does require permission. Answering a question by citing this book and quoting example code does not require permission. Incorporating a significant amount of example code from this book into your product's documentation does require permission.

We appreciate, but do not require, attribution. An attribution usually includes the title, author, publisher, and ISBN. For example: "*Just Spring Integration* by Madhusudhan Konda (O'Reilly). Copyright 2012 Madhusudhan Konda, 978-1-449-31608-2."

If you feel your use of code examples falls outside fair use or the permission given above, feel free to contact us at *permissions@oreilly.com*.

Safari® Books Online

Safari Books Online (*www.safaribooksonline.com*) is an on-demand digital library that delivers expert content in both book and video form from the world's leading authors in technology and business. Technology professionals, software developers, web designers, and business and creative professionals use Safari Books Online as their primary resource for research, problem solving, learning, and certification training.

Safari Books Online offers a range of product mixes and pricing programs for organizations, government agencies, and individuals. Subscribers have access to thousands of books, training videos, and prepublication manuscripts in one fully searchable database from publishers like O'Reilly Media, Prentice Hall Professional, Addison-Wesley Professional, Microsoft Press, Sams, Que, Peachpit Press, Focal Press, Cisco Press, John Wiley & Sons, Syngress, Morgan Kaufmann, IBM Redbooks, Packt, Adobe Press, FT Press, Apress, Manning, New Riders, McGraw-Hill, Jones & Bartlett, Course Technology, and dozens more. For more information about Safari Books Online, please visit us online.

How to Contact Us

Please address comments and questions concerning this book to the publisher:

> O'Reilly Media, Inc.
> 1005 Gravenstein Highway North
> Sebastopol, CA 95472
> 800-998-9938 (in the United States or Canada)
> 707-829-0515 (international or local)
> 707-829-0104 (fax)

We have a web page for this book, where we list errata, examples, and any additional information. You can access this page at:

> *http://oreil.ly/just-spring-integration*

To comment or ask technical questions about this book, send email to:

> *bookquestions@oreilly.com*

For more information about our books, courses, conferences, and news, see our website at *http://www.oreilly.com*.

Find us on Facebook: *http://facebook.com/oreilly*

Follow us on Twitter: *http://twitter.com/oreillymedia*

Watch us on YouTube: *http://www.youtube.com/oreillymedia*

To contact the author, please visit Madhusudhan Konda's website at:

http://www.madhusudhan.com

Follow the author on Twitter: *http://twitter.com/mkonda007*

Acknowledgments

I sincerely wish to thank my editors, Mike Loukides and Meghan Blanchette, for having faith in me and directing me when lost. Also to all of those at O'Reilly, especially Rachel Steely and Ed Stephenson, as well as Dan Fauxsmith, Maria Stallone, Rob Romano, and Karen Montgomery, for helping shape this book.

I also sincerely express my deepest gratitude to Josh Long, Greg Turnquist, and Sandro Mancuso for their helpful insights, reviews, and guidance.

A big thanks to goes to my family, especially to my loving wife, Jeannette, for being very patient and supportive throughout the time of writing this book. Also to my wonderful five-year-old son, Joshua, who sacrificed his free time, allowing me to write when I explained to him what I was doing. He likes the cover picture a lot!

I also thank my family in India for their wonderful support and love.

In memory of my loving Dad!

CHAPTER 1

Integration Fundamentals

Introduction

In an Enterprise world, applications talking to other applications is inevitable. Developing Enterprise applications can be a big challenge, especially when it involves working with a mixture of disparate systems. Organizations continuously search for higher productivity associated with lower costs in bringing any Enterprise applications to the table. Over the last few years, messaging has been adopted as one of the preferred choices for Enterprise application communications.

Implementing messaging solutions has become easier over the last few years, but the complexities of integration are still a big hurdle. Many frameworks were created to address the issues surrounding integration. One such framework from Spring developers is Spring Integration. It is designed to implement well-known Enterprise Application Integration (EAI) patterns. As a well-built framework, Spring Integration makes inter- and intra-application messaging a breeze.

In this chapter, we look into Enterprise Integration from a general standpoint. We discuss the problem space that Spring Integration Framework is addressing. We introduce the framework very briefly and analyze Spring Integration's role in creating a sound messaging solution.

Integration Strategies

You may have seen applications reading configuration from a file system, persisting data to a database, sending messages to an external client, publishing email, FTPing daily snapshots, and performing other routine tasks. Whether you know it or not, your application is talking to different systems—File System, Database, email, FTP, etc. You may even have developed some sort of adapter that will integrate your application with these external systems.

Integrating disparate systems is not an uncommon task. Before the advent of integration frameworks, there were common strategies in the integration space. The most popular strategies are:

- **Shared File Systems:** Two or more applications share a common file system; one may write to it while the other may poll the file system to read it. The sender and receiver are decoupled in this case. This solution certainly works, but has drawbacks like performance, reliability, and dependency on the File system.

- **Single Database:** In this strategy, applications share the data from a single database. One application writes data to the table while the other simply reads from the table. The drawback is that this setup forces applications to use a unified schema throughout the organization. Shared databases also pose a few other issues, such as network lag and lock contention.

- **Messaging:** This strategy mainly encourages and supports sender-receiver decoupling. A sender application sends a piece of data enclosed in a message to a messaging middleman and forgets about it. A consumer consumes the message whenever it can and begins its own workflow. One of the advantages of using Messaging as the medium is that the sender and receiver are decoupled completely. Also, the messages can be enriched, transformed, routed, and filtered before hitting the end channels.

We will examine the Messaging strategy and how Spring Integration gives us the tools to develop a full-fledged application.

Messaging Patterns

We all know that in our day-to-day life, there are some common problems that may have common solutions. In the messaging domain, too, you can observe such recurring problems and encounter some solutions to them. These common solutions are recorded as patterns. During the last couple of decades, formal patterns emerged for some of the recurring problems. Instead of reinventing the wheel, one could create the solutions using the approach laid out by these patterns. For example, to decouple the sender and receiver, one can introduce a Message pattern—the sender sends a message, while the receiver receives this message. Each party is unaware of the other.

Any messaging system has a few building blocks to work with, such as Messages, Channels, Transformers, etc. These are identified as patterns and discussed later in the chapter.

One pattern that might require a mention is the *pipes and filters* pattern.

Let's look at a very simple example to demonstrate this pattern—a Unix *pipeline* (|) command. Most of us should be familiar with this command.

The pipeline command, denoted by |, is used to combine several Unix commands to achieve a complex task. Although it looks simple, this example shows the powerful concept of the *pipes and filters* architecture.

Our requirement is to find the word count of *Just Spring* in the just-spring-titles.txt file. Run the command as shown below to achieve this:

```
mkonda$ cat just-spring-titles.txt | grep "Just Spring" | wc -l
```

Going into detail, the above command consists of three endpoints and two channels. The cat, grep, and wc are the endpoints while the pipe (|) acts as a channel.

The cat command displays the contents of the file. But the display, instead of being sent to the screen, is sent to the grep command using the pipe. The grep command then picks up the contents and searches for the *Just Spring* string. The result is then passed on to another command, wc, in this case. This simply displays the word count on the screen.

Note that these commands do not know anything about each other. These are small, narrowly focused tools that take in messages and publish them. They don't depend on each other's API and can be developed independently.

If you are familiar with JMS or distributed technologies, you may have heard of Enterprise Messaging. Your application talking to another application over the network can be considered an Enterprise application. You may have to use an application server to host these applications if you want to expose services so other applications can call the service according to their needs.

However, we can also introduce messaging to a standalone program that may run in a single process (single JVM). Spring Integration is one such framework for inter- and intra-application messaging.

While knowing these patterns will help you understand Spring Integration technology, it is not a requirement. The Spring Integration framework is developed to implement the patterns discussed in *Enterprise Integration Patterns* by Gregor Hohpe and Bobby Woolf. I would advise you to read this book to understand the EAI subject in depth.

Traditional Programming Model

Let's consider an application that loads Trades from an external system (File, in this example). The requirements of processing these Trades are as follows:

- Trades should be segregated based on Trade types (NEW, CANCEL, AMEND, etc).
- Trades are then processed accordingly and persisted.
- An auditor tool should be notified once the Trades are persisted.

These are typical application requirements. Usually, one can code them in a single component, as shown in the example below:

```
//Pseudo code
public class TradesLoader {
    private List<Trade> trades = null;
    ....
    public void start(){
      trades = loadTrades(tradesFile);

      (for Trade t: trades){
         processTrade(t);
         persistTrades(t);
         auditNotify(t);
      }
    }

    public void processTrade(Trade trade){
        if (t.getStatus().equalsIgnoreCase("new")) {
           processNewTrade();
        } else if (t.getStatus().equalsIgnoreCase("ammend")) {
           processAmmendTrade();
        } else {
           processOtherTrade();
        }
    }

    public void loadTrades(File fromFile){ .. }
    public void persistTrades(Trade trade){ .. }
    public void auditNotify(Trade trade){ .. }

    public static void main(String[] args) {
      new TradesLoader().start();
    }
}
```

The loadTrades method reads the file and transforms its content into a list of Trades. Each Trade is then sent through various actions, such as processing, persisting, and notifying, as shown in the snippet above.

The drawback of this model is that the process typically works sequentially. Please see Figure 1-1, which illustrates this model.

There is no harm in adopting this programming model, except that the component is tightly coupled to a business workflow. If we have to add another workflow, such as raising a notification for all big Trades or creating a task to collect Trade patterns, then we have to burn our keyboards writing more if-else statements.

Did you also notice that the above TradesLoader is doing too much work, instead of just doing its basic job of loading Trades?

In order to reduce its burden, we have to refactor it so it will only load Trades. Its responsibility should end once the loading is finished and is decoupled from doing other processes.

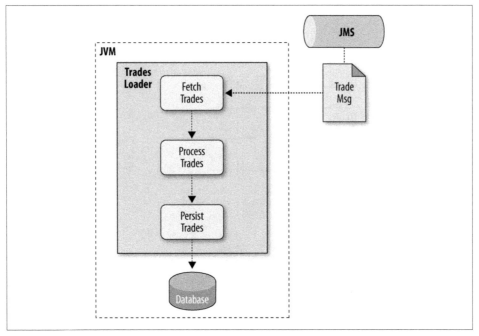

Figure 1-1. Serial Processing

So, how can we enhance the above `TradesLoader` to adapt to various scenarios that develop over a period of time?

One way is to use Messaging in our standalone application.

In this scenario, the `TradesLoader` fetches the Trades and posts them onto an internal data structure (a queue) before exiting. The relevant components, such as `TradeProcessor`, `TradePersistor`, and `TradeNotifier` will be working on their respective jobs to satisfy the workflow. They all can work at their own pace and not be bothered by the sequential processing anymore.

Standalone Messaging Model

The `TradesLoader` component can be refactored to do its job of loading the Trades from a file. In order to complete its task, the `TradesLoader` will publish the Trades to a data-holding structure like a bucket. In Messaging terms, this is called a *destination* or a *channel*. The rest of the components should be picking up the Trades from this channel, which acts as a conduit.

Note that we did not introduce a full-blown enterprise messaging solution here. It would be overkill, because it would introduce a whole stack of infrastructure and open doors to different programming models.

See Figure 1-2, which depicts a sort of parallel process using a standalone messaging model.

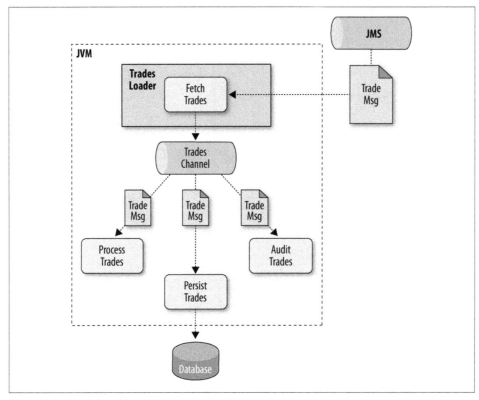

Figure 1-2. Standalone Messaging

The Spring Integration framework is an excellent choice for this type of messaging solution. If you are already familiar with Spring Framework or if your project is already *springified*, then you are in good hands. Spring Integration is perceived as an extension of the Spring Core, so you will obtain all the benefits of dependency injection, decoupling, testability, etc. You do not need to have an application server to host your messaging solution when you use Spring Integration—which is a big advantage, as you don't have to invest time and money in adopting the messaging technologies.

We will look at the framework in detail in the next chapter.

Summary

This chapter has scratched the surface of Enterprise integration fundamentals. It introduced messaging strategy patterns. It touched the pipes and filters pattern upon which Spring Integration Framework is based. It also discussed the sequential processing programming model against the standalone messaging mode. It set the scene for the in-depth coverage of the framework in the coming chapters.

CHAPTER 2

Basics

Introduction

The Spring Integration framework is built on a few basic building blocks—Messages, Channels, and Endpoints. Messages are the containers of data, while channels are the addresses holding these messages. Endpoints are components that connect to the channels to consume or publish messages. The next few chapters will discuss these building blocks at length, but we'll touch on them in this chapter, as well.

The `Message` component is discussed here, while the rest of the components (channels, endpoints, etc.) will be discussed in their own chapters later on.

Messages

Messages are the objects that carry information between two applications. They are constructed at one end, usually the producer side of the messaging application. They are then consumed and deconstructed at the other end, the consumer/subscriber side. Think of the message as an object that carries business data, such a new `Account` or `Trade` information. The publisher/producer creates these objects and publishes them to a channel. A subscriber/consumer connected to the same channel then receives those messages. The domain objects are then resurrected from these messages, and business processing is carried out.

Dissecting a Message

The Message consists of two parts—the `payload` and `header` properties.

Imagine a greeting card arriving in your mailbox on your birthday. The card inside the envelope may be called the `payload`. Payload is the data or the information that has to be processed by the interested parties. The greeting card also has some additional information—the sender's and receiver's addresses, first- or second-class delivery, and possibly instructions such as "Handle with Care." Such additional pieces of information are header properties.

The payload and header properties are represented as a Message interface in Spring Integration, as shown below:

```
public interface Message<T> {
  T getPayLoad();
  MessageHeaders getHeaders();
}
```

Figure 2-1 depicts the TradeMessage composition.

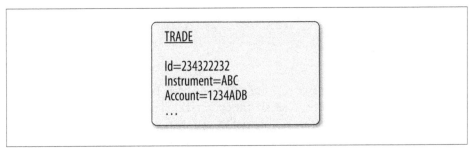

Figure 2-1. Message Composition

From the above definition of a Message, you can set any *Plain Old Java Object* (POJO) as a payload. If you are familiar with JMS, you will remember that the payload object should be serializable.

In Spring Integration's world, this restriction is lifted. However, the MessageHeaders class will implement a Serializable interface:

```
public final class MessageHeaders
  implements Map<String, Object>, Serializable { ... }
```

As shown in the above definition, headers take the set of properties as string value pairs.

In the Account example, the details of the account such as name, address, initial balance, etc., form the part of the payload. The header constitutes name-value pairs of properties such as which channel to be sent to, what type of priority to associate with it, etc.

Generic Implementation

Framework provides a concrete implementation of the Message interface called GenericMessage. You can create an instance of GenericMessage using one of the two provided constructors—one with payload and the other with payload and header properties. However, you are strongly advised to use a utility class MessageBuilder instead. The following snippet demonstrates this:

```
// Create payload object
Account a = new Account();
```

```
// creating a map with header properties
Map<String, Object> accountProperties
  = new HashMap<String, Object>();

// Set our header properties
accountProperties.put("ACCOUNT_EXPIRY","NEVER");

// Use MessageBuilder class to create a Message
// and set header properties

Message<Account> m =
  MessageBuilder.withPayload(a)
  .setHeader("ACCOUNT_EXPIRY", "NEVER")
  .build();
```

The MessageBuilder utility class is used to create and manipulate Message and its headers. This class follows the builder pattern.

Message Channels

While Message represents a container for information data, the channel represents the location where it is being sent. Simply put, the message ends up at a prespecified address called channel before being used by someone else. The sender and receiver will be encoded with the information of the channels. See Figure 2-2, depicting the Message channels. In Spring Integration, the channel is represented by a MessageChannel interface.

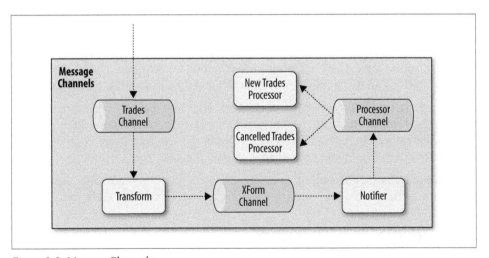

Figure 2-2. Message Channels

Declaring Channels

Spring Integration provides a declarative model to create channels so we don't have to instantiate channels using Java classes. Declaring a channel is simple and straightforward, as shown in the following snippet:

```
<beans
  xmlns:int="http://www.springframework.org/schema/integration"
  xsi:schemaLocation="http://www.springframework.org/schema/integration
    http://www.springframework.org/schema/integration/spring-integration-2.1.xsd"
  ...
  >

  // declaratively creating a channel
  <int:channel id="newAccounts">
</beans>
```

Note that since the channels, along with other messaging components, are defined in the integration XML namespace, please make sure your XML file consists of the above namespaces.

Out of the box, the framework provides a few concrete implementations, such as QueueChannel, PriorityChannel, and RendezvousChannel. Although there are a few differences among all the channel implementations, the underlying principle is to behave as an address for an endpoint. We will discuss channels in the next chapter.

Endpoints

Endpoints are basically components that consume messages from an input channel and deliver to an output channel. They may only consume messages from an input channel or only produce messages to an output channel. They are the crucial pieces that combine our business logic with integration specifications. The message endpoints are created declaratively so that applications concentrate on their business logic alone.

The Framework provides several out-of-the-box endpoints such as Transformers, Splitters, Filters, Routers, etc. It also provides endpoints (adapters) that connect to external systems like JMS, FTP, JDBC, Twitter, etc. You can also extend and create an Endpoint if you have a new requirement for an adapter fetching data from the moon.

We will be discussing the endpoints in later chapters, but if you are eager to see endpoints in action, here's an example of declaring a Service Activator endpoint.

Service Activator Endpoint Example

A Service Activator is a generic endpoint that invokes a method on a bean when a message arrives at an input channel. Declaration of the endpoint is shown in the following snippet:

```
<int:service-activator input-channel="positions-channel"
                        ref="newPositionProcessor"
                        method="processNewPosition">
</int:service-activator>

// bean to be invoked
<bean id="newPositionProcessor"
class="com.madhusudhan.jsi.basics.NewPositionProcessor" />
```

The `service-activator` endpoint picks up a message as soon as it arrives on the `positions-channel` and calls the `processNewPosition` method on the bean. Any code required to fetch messages or invoke the bean's method is already included in the `service-activator` snippet. This is the power of the framework.

Example

Now that we have seen the various building blocks of the framework, let's see a working example. Don't worry too much if the components appearing in the example don't makes sense. You will understand all of them as we progess through the book.

A Trader may use a web application to place a Trade. The Trades are sent to a JMS destination, where they are processed by another component to book the Trades. The requirement is to connect to a JMS Destination and fetch the Trades and process them.

The Spring Integration framework helps you focus on coding the business logic while it handles the mundane tasks. You can use an adapter (`inbound-channel-adapter`) to pick up the messages from an input JMS Queue. The declaration of the adapter is given below:

```
<int:channel id="trades-channel"/>

<jms:inbound-channel-adapter id="tradesJmsAdapter"
  connection-factory="connectionFactory"
  destination="tradesQueue"
  channel="trades-channel">

  <int:poller fixed-rate="1000" />
</jms:inbound-channel-adapter>

<bean id="tradesQueue"
  class="org.apache.activemq.command.ActiveMQQueue">
  <constructor-arg value="TRADES_QUEUE" />
</bean>

<bean name="connectionFactory" class="org.apache.activemq.ActiveMQConnectionFactory">
  <property name="brokerURL">
    <value>tcp://localhost:61616</value>
  </property>
</bean>
```

The `inbound-channel-adapter` element declaration takes away all the boilerplate code. It makes a connection to the JMS Destination, fetches the data from `positionsQueue`, converts the message to our internal format, and finally publishes the Trades to our internal channel, `trades-channel`. The `connection-factory` element provides the necessary information on where the endpoint should connect to fetch the messages (in this case, an AMQ server running on `localhost`).

Now, we wire in a `Service Activator` endpoint to be invoked for every new `Trade` message. This endpoint simply picks up the incoming message from `trades-channel` and invokes the `processNewTrade` method on `NewTradeProcessor` bean.

```
<int:service-activator
  input-channel="trades-channel"
  ref="newTradeProcessor"
  method="processNewTrade">
</int:service-activator>

// bean that would be invoked
<bean id="newTradeProcessor"
  class="com.madhusudhan.jsi.basics.NewTradeProcessor" />
```

Next, we write a simple Java class `NewTradeProcessor` with a `processNewTrade` method that takes in the `Trade` message:

```
public class NewTradeProcessor {

  public void processNewTrade(Trade t){
    // Process your trade here.
    System.out.println("Message received:"+m.getPayload().toString());
  }
}
```

Write a test class that loads this XML file and publishes a dummy Trade as shown below:

```
public class NewTradeProcessorTest {
  private ApplicationContext ctx = null;
  private MessageChannel channel = null;

  // Constructor which instantiates the endpoints
  public NewTradeProcessorTest() {
    ctx = new ClassPathXmlApplicationContext("basics-example-beans.xml");
    channel = ctx.getBean("trades-channel", MessageChannel.class);
  }

  private Trade createNewTrade() {
    Trade t = new Trade();
    t.setId("1234");
    ...
    return t;
  }

  private void sendTrade() {
    Trade trade = createNewTrade();
    Message<Trade> tradeMsg =
      MessageBuilder.withPayload(trade).build();
    channel.send(tradeMsg, 10000);
```

```
    System.out.println("Trade Message published.");
  }

  public static void main(String[] args) {
    NewTradeProcessorTest test = new NewTradeProcessorTest();
    test.sendTrade();
  }
}
```

The framework provides endpoints that can be configured using XML notations that will take away the bulk of the work. Instead of writing code, we use the declarative model.

Summary

This chapter has given you an overview of the goals of the Spring Integration framework. It introduced the basic building blocks of the framework—the messages, channels, and endpoints. The chapter explained the fundamentals by providing simple examples.

CHAPTER 3

Message Channels

Introduction

We all have a postal address where presents from Santa may end up (if he mails them, of course) for Christmas. Message channels resemble such addresses where the messages will be sent or received. Producers and consumers do not talk to each other directly but communicate via these channels. The decoupling of the sender and receiver components is primarily achieved by using channels. Channels represent pipes in our pipes and filters pattern. You can create a complex integration solution consisting of channels and endpoints.

This chapter mainly focuses on configuring and using these channels.

Message Channels

We have seen in the previous chapter that the `MessageChannel` interface has methods to send data using a `Message` object.

```
boolean send(Message message);
boolean send(Message message, long timeout)
```

Both the methods above will take the `Message` as a parameter. The first method publishes the message but does not return control until it successfully executes the sending operation. This is not desirable due to wastage of CPU cycles. In this situation, the second `send` method takes over. When the message is not delivered for whatever reason after a predefined time, the second method steps in and throws an exception.

Note the return value of these methods, `boolean`, indicates the success or failure of the message delivery.

The timeout variable can be set to zero, positive, or negative values.

If the timeout variable is negative, the thread will block indefinitely until it is able to publish the message successfully. If it is set to zero, the `send` method will return instantly, whether the sending was successful or not. If it is greater than zero, the sending thread will honor that amount of time before throwing an error if it is unable to push the message to the channel.

The interesting point is that the MessageChannel interface does not define any methods for receiving messages. Receiving a message largely depends on the receiver's semantics: *Point-to-Point (P2P)* or *Publish/Subscribe (Pub/Sub)*.

In a P2P mode, only one receiver will get the message delivered, even if multiple receivers are connected to that channel. It is valid to have more than one consumer connected to a channel, but the consumer may be selected randomly (or using a round-robin strategy). In a pub-sub mode, the message is delivered to all consumers who have subscribed to that channel. This means that each message is copied and provided to the subscribers.

There's one more thing to consider: *message buffering*. The incoming messages are buffered in order to stop flooding the consumers. The messages are kept in a queue—in internal memory or to a durable storage area, depending on the configuration. There are ways of persisting the messages onto a durable storage area, which we will see in coming chapters.

So, the takeaway point is—clients choose the channels depending on delivery mode (P2P or Pub/Sub) and buffering or non-buffering semantics. There are two separate interfaces that deal with the receiving side of messages.

Receiving Messages

The Spring Integration framework exposes the delivery modes using two separate interfaces—PollableChannel and SubscribableChannel. As both of them extend the MessageChannel, the send methods are automatically inherited.

Point-to-Point Mode

In a P2P mode, the consumer can simply use any of the PollableChannel implementations.

The following code snippet illustrates the PollableChannel interface:

```
public interface PollableChannel extends MessageChannel {
  // This call blocks the thread until it receives a message
  Message<?> receive();

  // This call will wait for a specified timeout before
  // throwing a failure if message is not available
  Message<?> receive(long timeout);
}
```

There are two receive methods, one with and the other without a timeout. The method without timeout blocks forever, so use this method with caution; the other method waits for a predefined time and exits if a message is not found.

Out of the box, the framework provides such concrete implementations as QueueChannel, PriorityChannel, and RendezvousChannel. As the name indicates, QueueChannel also has the capability of buffering the messages. PriorityChannel and RendezvousChannel are finer implementations of the QueueChannel and they exhibit P2P and buffering characteristics.

Instead of creating these concrete classes in Java code, the Spring container can create them when the application starts.

P2P Example

The following code demonstrates the process of receiving messages in P2P mode:

```
public class QueueChannelTest {
  private ApplicationContext ctx = null;
  private MessageChannel qChannel = null;

  public QueueChannelTest() {
    ctx = new ClassPathXmlApplicationContext("channels-beans.xml");
    qChannel = ctx.getBean("q-channel", MessageChannel.class);
  }
  public void receive() {
    // This method receives a message, however it blocks
    // indefinitely until it finds a message
    // Message m = ((QueueChannel) qChannel).receive();

    // This method receives a message, however it exists
    // within the 10 seconds even if doesn't find a message
    Message m = ((QueueChannel) qChannel).receive(10000);
    System.out.println("Payload: " + m.getPayload());
  }
}
```

Using the receive method without a timeout may incur the following consequence: until a message appears on the channel, the current thread will block indefinitely. While the second method attempts to receive a message from the channel, it will quit if the message doesn't appear within the predefined time (10 seconds in the example), thus saving the CPU cycles.

You can also indicate zero as the timeout to the receive method, which means the method returns immediately even if it can't find the message. Supplying a negative timeout will also block a call—it is as good as using the receive method without a timeout.

The channels-beans.xml is the configuration file that has the definition of our queue-channel, as shown here:

```
<int:channel id="q-channel">
  <int:queue capacity="10" />
</int:channel>
```

The queue-channel is set with a capacity of 10 elements. There are various implementations of the channel, which we will see shortly.

Pub/Sub Mode

For receiving messages in Pub/Sub mode, use `SubscribableChannel`. As described earlier, each message will be broadcast to all registered subscribers. In this mode, all subscribers will receive the message before it is removed from the channel. By contrast, in P2P mode, many consumers may have registered with the channel, but only a single subscriber will be selected to process the message.

The following code snippet illustrates the `SubscribableChannel` interface definition:

```
public interface SubscribableChannel extends MessageChannel {
  // to subscribe a MessageHandler for handling the messages
  boolean subscribe(MessageHandler handler);

  // unsubscribe
  boolean unsubscribe(MessageHandler handler);
}
```

The interface has two methods, one to subscribe and another to unsubscribe a `MessageHandler`. A `MessageHandler` is an instance provided by the client to process incoming messages. For each channel, zero or many handlers are registered by the client. For every message that appears on the channel, the framework delivers each message to the registered handlers by invoking the only method, `handleMessage()`:

```
public interface MessageHandler{

  // this method is invoked when a fresh message appears on the channel
  void handleMessage(Message<?> message) throws MessagingException;

}
```

The `handleMessage` is where the application holds the logic to process the incoming message.

Pub/Sub Example

Let's see an example of the Pub/Sub mode of reception. The following snippet demonstrates this example:

```
public class ChannelTest {
  private ApplicationContext ctx = null;
  private MessageChannel pubSubChannel = null;

  public ChannelTest() {
    ctx = new ClassPathXmlApplicationContext("channels-beans.xml");
    pubSubChannel = ctx.getBean("pubsub-channel", MessageChannel.class);
  }

  public void subscribe() {
    ((PublishSubscribeChannel)pubSubChannel).subscribe(new TradeMessageHandler());
  }

  class TradeMessageHandler implements MessageHandler {
    public void handleMessage(Message<?> message) throws MessagingException {
```

```
    System.out.println("Handling Message:" + message);
    }
  }
}
```

The `TradeMessageHandler` is the handler class that is subscribed to the `pubsub-channel`. It implements the `MessageHandler` interface. The framework invokes the `handleMessage()` method for any incoming messages. Ideally, this is the entry point to our client.

When a message arrives on the `pubsub-channel`, the following output is the result:

```
Handling Message:[Payload=Trade [id=1234, direction=BUY,
    account=B12D45,security=null, status=NEW]]
    [Headers={timestamp=1328090013863, id=d144f752-a846-468c-a4c3-0a265f3062ff}]
```

The payload and headers of the message are printed out onto the console. The payload of the message is `Trade` and the `toString()` method is invoked.

The configuration of the channel in the XML file is simple: the `publish-subscribe-channel` tag represents a `PublishSubscribeChannel` shown below:

```
<int:publish-subscribe-channel id="pubsub-channel"/>
```

Now that we have seen the high level usage of channels, let's look at the various implementations.

Queue Channel

This channel exhibits Point-to-Point characteristics—meaning only one consumer will receive the message—but remember, there is no restriction for creating multiple consumers here. This channel also supports buffering messages as it uses a queue data structure to hold the messages in memory. As it implements a queue, there is a capacity associated with it. Note that the default constructor without a capacity parameter creates a channel with unbounded capacity.

The channel is declared using integration namespace support as shown below:

```
<int:channel id="newAccounts">
  <int:queue capacity="100"/>
</int:channel>
```

The above configuration creates a `Queue` channel with a capacity for 100 elements. If you omit the queue capacity, the channel will be created with an unlimited capacity. Take extra care when creating unlimited capacity channels as they will drain your application's memory. If capacity is not provided, `Integer.MAX_VALUE` is assumed as its capacity.

What happens to the sender if there is no room for any additional messages to be published? This can happen if the consumer is slow or dead. The queue will fill up, as no consumer is consuming the messages. In this case, the sender will either be blocked until space is available or timeout occurs, depending on the send method used (please see Figure 2-2 for an explanation of message sending).

Note that the QueueChannel implements *First In First Out* (FIFO) ordering. The data structure in the backend is a standard java.util.concurrent.LinkedBlockingQueue implementation.

The QueueChannel also provides a method to purge the channel with a predefined selection criteria via the MessageSelector implementation:

```
public List<Message<?>> purge(MessageSelector selector){ .. }
```

To purge the channel completely, simply pass null as the selector to the method. This will wipe off the whole queue.

Priority Channel

The PriorityChannel is a subclass of QueueChannel with just one additional characteristic—prioritization of messages. If you need to send a high-priority message immediately, then PriorityChannel is the one to use. The easiest way is to set the PRIORITY property on the MessageHeader when creating a message.

Let's look at an example to create a message with priority. The publishPriorityTrade method publishes a new Trade onto the provided channel. Priority of the message is set by using the MessageHeader's PRIORITY property. Its value is an integer, thus the higher the value, the higher the priority.

```
public void publishPriorityTrade(Trade t) {
  Message<Trade> tradeMsg = MessageBuilder.withPayload(t).
    setHeader(MessageHeades.PRIORITY, 10).build();

  priorityChannel.send(tradeMsg, 10000);

  System.out.println("The Message is published successfully");
}
```

Messages with a higher priority will end up at the top of the queue, while the lower-priority messages will be pushed down. The default behavior is to use MessageHeaders' PRIORITY property to sort the messages.

In order to create a priority channel, use the priority-queue element as shown in the following XML code:

```
<int:channel id="newAccounts">
  <int:priority-queue capacity="10" />
</int:channel>
```

The priority-queue tag lets the framework create a PriorityChannel with a given capacity.

If you need to further customize priorities, you need to provide your own comparator by implementing Comparator<Message<?>> to the constructor. The following code snippet shows the AccountComparator:

```
public class AccountComparator implements Comparator<Message<Account>> {

  @Override
  public int compare(Message<Account> msg1, Message<Account> msg2) {
    Account a1 = (Account)msg1.getPayload();
    Account a2 = (Account)msg2.getPayload();

    Integer i1 = a1.getAccountType();
    Integer i2 = a2.getAccountType();

    return i1.compareTo(i2);
  }
}
```

Once you define the Comparator, you need to let the framework know you are going to use it for all the messages coming into the priority channel. You do this by using the comparator tag:

```
<int:channel id="newAccounts">
  <int:priority-queue capacity="10" comparator="accountComparator"/>
</int:channel>

<bean id="accountComparator" class="com.madhusudhan.jsi.channels.AccountComparator"/>
```

The priority-queue expects capacity and comparator values. In the above snippet, we set the AccountComparator as the comparator on the channel.

Rendezvous Channel

Rendezvous Channel is a subclass of QueueChannel, and exhibits P2P characteristics. Unlike QueueChannel, it implements a zero capacity queue. In the backend, it uses a SynchronousQueue data structure. This means that at any time, only one message can exist on the channel. When a producer sends a message, it will block until that message is consumed by the consumer. Similarly, a consumer will be blocked until a message appears on the channel.

You define the rendezvous channel in your XML config using rendezvous-queue, as shown below:

```
<int:channel id="newAccounts">
  <int:rendezvous-queue/>
</int:channel>
```

The RendezvousChannel is ideal when you wish to receive a reply for your request. The client will post a request message with a property in the message headers as a reply channel:

```
public void sendTradeToRendezvous(Trade t) {
  Message<Trade> tradeMsg = MessageBuilder.withPayload(t).
```

```
  .setHeader(MessageHeaders.REPLY_CHANNEL, "replyChannel").build();
  rendezvousChannel.send(tradeMsg, 10000);
  System.out.println(t.getStatus()
    + " Trade published to a Rendezvous channel");
}
```

Once the message is received, the consumer inspects the header to see if a reply needs to be sent to a REPLY_CHANNEL.

```
Message m =
  ((RendezvousChannel) rendezvousChannel).receive(10000);

//get the reply channel
MessageChannel replyChannel =
  (MessageChannel) m.getHeaders().get(MessageHeaders.REPLY_CHANNEL);

//send a reply to it
replyChannel.send(..);
```

PublishSubscribe Channel

Use PublishSubscribeChannel if you need to send a message to multiple consumers. This is the implementation of the SubscribableChannel interface out of the box. There are no receive methods in this channel because the message reception is handled by a subscriber called MessageHandler.

The declaration of the channel in an XML config file is simple and straightforward:

```
<int:publish-subscribe-channel id="newAccounts" />
```

The publish-subscribe-channel tag identifies the channel as PublishSubcribeChannel. Once you have a reference to the channel, you need to set a handler:

```
public class PubSubTest{
  MessageHandler handler = new TradeMessageHandler();
  private ApplicationContext ctx = null;
  private PublishSubscribeChannel pubSubChannel = null;
  ...
  // subscribe to the channel
  public void subscribe() {
    boolean handlerAdded = pubSubChannel.subscribe(handler);
    System.out.println("Handler added?" + handlerAdded);
  }

  // Unsubscribe using the same channel and handler references.
  public void unsubscribe() {
    boolean handlerRemoved = pubSubChannel.unsubscribe(handler);
    System.out.println("Handler removed?" + handlerRemoved);
  }

  //Handler to handle the messages
  class TradeMessageHandler implements MessageHandler {
    public void handleMessage(Message<?> message) throws MessagingException {
      System.out.println("Handling Message:" + message);
    }
```

```
    }
}
```

When a message appears on the channel, it invokes the registered handler passing on the message for further processing.

Direct Channel

DirectChannel is a mixed type channel with both P2P and Pub/Sub characteristics. It implements SubscribableChannel so you need to have a concrete implementation of MessageHandler subscribing to it. Messages can be consumed by subscribed handlers, but only one subscriber will be getting each message, thus displaying P2P semantics. Even if you have registered multiple subscribers, the channel will deliver to only one of them. The framework uses the round-robin strategy to choose a recipient from the multiple subscribers.

The production and consumption of the message are both executed in the same thread. This usage is very helpful for Enterprise applications with transactions spanning multiple resources.

With no additional overhead for its creation, this channel is chosen to be a default channel. We have already seen in our earlier examples how the channel is defined in XML:

```
<int:channel id="newAccounts"/>
```

If multiple handlers are subscribed to the channel, these two questions—which subscriber will be chosen to process the message and what happens if a chosen handler is unable to process the message—will be answered by the load-balancer and failover properties.

The load-balancer flag chooses an appropriate load-balancing strategy to select one of the handlers. The out-of-the-box strategy is the round-robin strategy.

The failover property is a Boolean flag. If set to true, it will let the subsequent handlers process the messages if the initial chosen handler throws an exception while handling the messages for whatever reason. By default, the failover flag is set to true.

Because the DirectChannel delegates its functionality of handling subscribers to a MessageDispatcher, both properties are set on a dispatcher attribute:

```
<int:channel id="newAccounts">
  <dispatcher failover="false" load-balancer="round-robin"/>
</int:channel>
```

Note that the load-balancer on the channel is by default set to the round-robin strategy, so you do not have to declare as shown above. If you wish to ignore the load-balancing strategy, set the load-balancer to none value.

Executor Channel

The `ExecutorChannel` implements `SubscribableChannel` and is similar to the `DirectChannel`, except that the dispatching of the message is carried by a `java.uti.con current.Executor` instance. Unlike the `sending` thread taking full control in `DirectChannel` implementation, the `send` thread completes its execution after publishing the message in `ExecutorChannel`. The consumption of the message is processed in a separate thread handled by the dispatcher. The dispatcher invokes the executor for message processing by the consumer.

```
<int:channel id="newAccounts">
  <int:dispatcher task-executor="accountsExecutor"/>
</int:channel>

// define the executor
<bean id="accountsExecutor"
  class="com.madhusudhan.jsi.channels.AccountsExecutor"/>
```

You can set a load-balancing strategy and failover using the `load-balancer` and `fail over` attributes on `dispatcher` as we did on `DirectChannel`. The default values are round-robin strategy with `failover` enabled.

```
<int:channel id="newAccounts">
  <int:dispatcher load-balancer="none"
  failover="false"
  task-executor="accountsExecutor"/>
</int:channel>
```

Null Channel

The `Null Channel` is `PollableChannel` used primarily for testing purposes. The sending methods always return `true`, indicating the operation is successful, while the receiving methods always get a `null` message. Internally, the code does not create any queues, but returns `true` on a `send` operation or `null` on a `receive` operation immediately. For the complete picture (and if you are curious like me), see the actual implementation of the `send` and `receive` methods in the framework:

```
// This is the framework class implementation
public class NullChannel implements PollableChannel {
  // send will always return true
  public boolean send(Message<?> message) {
    if (logger.isDebugEnabled()) {
      logger.debug("message sent to null channel: " + message);
    }
    return true;
  }

  // receive will return null always
  public Message<?> receive() {
    if (logger.isDebugEnabled()) {
      logger.debug("receive called on null channel");
    }
```

```
        return null;
    }
    ...
}
```

Summary

Message channels are the primary components that separate producers from consumers. This chapter explained the various message channels in detail. The channels that one should select depend on either P2P or Pub/Sub nature. In a P2P, only one consumer receives, while in a Pub/Sub model, all registered subscribers receive a copy of the message. In addition, Spring Integration provides a functionality for buffering the messages in order to avoid over-flooding the consumers. The various out-of-the-box implementations of channels cater to these characteristics.

CHAPTER 4

Endpoints

Introduction

A well-designed messaging application separates business logic from integration details. The application code concentrates on implementing the business logic. The connection mechanism, the message sending and receiving and other aspects of messaging are hidden from the application. It would be a good design to implement them using declarative programming so the program behavior can be altered based on the changing needs of the business.

Message Endpoints are components that separate business logic from the messaging framework. They are crucial in the integration space for hiding the messaging details. They are responsible for connecting application components to the messaging channels to send or receive messages.

Spring Integration provides endpoints such as Service Activators, Channel Adapters, Message Bridges, Gateways, Transformers, Filters, and Routers. This chapter introduces common endpoints such as Service Activators, Channel Adapters, Message Bridges, and Gateways, while the following chapters discuss Transformers, Filters, Aggregators, Routers, and the rest.

If you are interested in the framework's classes designed to create these endpoints, then you should read the *"For the Curious: Endpoint API" on page 38* section at the end of this chapter. It discusses in detail the inner workings of these endpoints. Note that you will not be required to use these API classes in your code. You should use the declarative model and appropriate namespaces to configure these endpoints.

Common Endpoints

We have touched upon one of the common endpoints in an earlier chapter—Service Activators. In this section, we will discuss this in detail, and other endpoints, too. First, make sure that you have the `integration` namespace declared in your XML file for these endpoints:

```
...
xmlns:int="http://www.springframework.org/schema/integration"

xsi:schemaLocation="http://www.springframework.org/schema/integration
  http://www.springframework.org/schema/integration/spring-integration-2.1.xsd"
...
```

Service Activator

The Service Activator is a generic endpoint which invokes a method on a bean whenever a message arrives on the channel. If the method has a return value, then the value will be sent to an output channel if the channel is configured.

Configuring the activator using the namespace is relatively straightforward. Use the service-activator element, setting input-channel and a ref to the bean:

```
<int:service-activator
  input-channel="positions-channel"
  ref="newTradeActivator"
  method="processNewPosition">
</int:service-activator>

<bean id="newTradeActivator"
  class="com.madhusudhan.jsi.endpoints.common.NewTradeActivator" />
```

Any message arriving at positions-channel will be passed on to a NewTradeActivator (which the attribute ref points to) and the processNewPosition method is invoked which is declared using the method attribute. If the bean class has only one method, then you do not have to declare the method attribute—the framework resolves it as the service method and invokes it appropriately.

The NewTradeActivator is a simple class that has a single method which expects a Position object. This class is basically the entry point to acting as a service.

```
public class NewTradeActivator {
  Position position = ..
  public void processNewPosition(Position t) {
    System.out.println("Method invoked to process the new Position"+t);
    // process the position..
    // ...
  }
}
```

The method can return a non-null value which is wrapped in a Message and sent to an output-channel. For example, if you wish to send a reply to another channel after processing the Position, you can do this by simply returning the position as the method's return value:

```
// Return value will be wrapped in a Message
// and sent to an output channel
public Position processNewPosition(Position t) {
  System.out.println("Method invoked to process the new Position"+t);
  // process the position..
```

```
// ...
    return position;
}
```

You may omit declaring the optional `output-channel` attribute. If you do, and if your method has a return value, then the framework will use the message header property called `replyChannel` to send the reply. An exception will be thrown if no `replyChannel` header property is found.

The service method can have either `Message` or a Java object as an argument. In the latter case, the payload from the incoming message is extracted and passed on to the message. As the incoming message is a Java Object, this mode will not tie our implementation to Spring API, making it a preferred option. In the above example, a `Position` is wrapped up in a `Message` and sent to the channel.

Message Bridge

A `MessageBridge` is a simple endpoint that couples different messaging modes or adapters. An example of a common use of the bridge is to tie up a `point-to-point` (P2P) mode channel to a `Publish/Subscribe` (Pub/Sub) mode. In a `P2P` mode, a `PollableChannel` is used by the endpoint, whereas a `PublishSubscribeChannel` is used in `Pub/Sub` mode.

The `MessageBridge` is declared using the `bridge` element in the integration namespace:

```
<int:publish-subscribe-channel
  id="trades-in-channel" />

<int:channel id="trades-out-channel">
  <int:queue capacity="10" />
</int:channel>

<!-- Bridges pub/sub channel to a p2p channel -->

<int:bridge input-channel="trades-in-channel"
        output-channel="trades-out-channel" />
```

In the above snippet, the bridge picks up a message from the input channel and publishes onto the output channel. The input channel is `PublishSubscribeChannel`, while the output channel is `QueueChannel`.

To complete our example, a service activator is hooked onto the output channel. As soon as the message arrives at the output channel (via the bridge endpoint), the `PositionReceiver` bean is invoked for action:

```
<int:service-activator
  input-channel="trades-out-channel"
  ref="positionReceiver"/>

<bean id="positionReceiver"
  class="com.madhusudhan.jsi.endpoints.PositionReceiver"/>
```

Message Enricher

A `Message Enricher` component enriches the incoming message with additional information and sends the updated object to the downstream consumers. For example, a Trade normally consists of a piece of coded information, such as a security ID or a customer account number. The reason for this is not only to keep the `Trade` object slim and sleek, but also to protect the confidential information from other systems. This data is attached while the Trade passes through different stages as and when required.

The Framework provides two types for enriching messages: `Header Enricher` and `Pay load Enricher`.

Header Enricher

You can add additional header attributes to the message using the `Header Enricher` component. Let's say the incoming `Trade` message needs to have a couple of header properties: `SRC_SYSTEM` and `TARGET_SYSTEM`. As these properties were not in the original message, the message needs to be enriched. We use the `header-enricher` tag to do this:

```
<int:header-enricher
  input-channel="in-channel"
  output-channel="out-channel">
  <int:header name="SRC_SYSTEM" value="BBG" />
  <int:header name="TARGET_SYSTEM" value="LOCAL" />

</int:header-enricher>
```

As you can see, we added two properties to the outgoing message. So, if you print out the headers of this message, the newly added properties should appear on the console:

```
Headers: {timestamp=1328187611172,
  SRC_SYSTEM=BBG, TARGET_SYSTEM=LOCAL, id=...}
```

You can set a number of predefined properties such as `priority`, `reply-channel`, `error-channel`, etc.

This is the enhanced configuration for `header-enricher`:

```
<int:header-enricher id="maxi-enricher" input-channel="in-channel"
  output-channel="out-channel">
    <int:priority value="10"/>
    <int:error-channel ref="myErrorChannel"/>
    <int:correlation-id value="APP_OWN_ID"/>
    <int:reply-channel value="reply-channel"/>
    <int:header name="SRC_SYSTEM" value="BBG" />
</int:header-enricher>

<int:publish-subscribe-channel id="myErrorChannel" />
```

Note that the `ref` tag looks for a named bean while the `value` tag takes a literal value only.

Framework also supports setting header properties using `payload` by allowing the `header-enricher`'s header property to refer to a bean:

```
<int:header-enricher id="pojo-enricher"
  input-channel="in-channel"
  output-channel="out-channel">
  <int:header name="ID"
  ref="tradeEnricher" method="enrichHeader"/>
</int:header-enricher>
```

The ID is set by extracting data from the payload with the help of the TradeEnricher bean. The following snippet shows this bean, which has a simple functionality in returning the ID attribute by reading the Trade's ID and adding SRC to it at the end.

```
public class TradeEnricher {
  public String enrichHeader(Message m) {
    Trade t = (Trade)m.getPayload();
    return t.getId()+"SRC";
  }
}
```

Payload Enricher

If the requirement is to add or enrich the payload with additional information, use the PayloadEnricher component. The enricher tag in the integration namespace is used to configure the payload enricher. The workings of a payload enricher require a closer look.

Let's see the configuration first:

```
<int:enricher input-channel="in-channel"
  request-channel="enricher-req-channel"
  output-channel="stdout">
  <int:property name="price" expression="payload.price"/>
  <int:property name="instrument" expression="payload.instrument"/>
</int:enricher>

<int:service-activator input-channel="enricher-req-channel"
  ref="tradeEnricher">
</int:service-activator>

<bean id="enricherBean" class="com.madhusudhan.jsi.endpoints.enricher.Enricher" />
<bean id="tradeEnricher"
class="com.madhusudhan.jsi.endpoints.enricher.PriceEnricher" />
```

There's a lot going on here. Like any other endpoint, the enricher expects a message in the input-channel, too. It picks up the message and passes it on to request-channel and waits for a reply. There should be some other component listening on this request-channel to enrich the message. After enriching the payload, this component then publishes the reply back to the reply channel. The reply channel is declared as a header property on the message itself (see the Price Message below). Once the enricher gets a reply, it sets the properties with the enriched data by using expressions (See "Spring Expressions" on page 37 later in this chapter for details about expressions).

In the above configuration, a Price is posted onto the in-channel. The Price message does not have any data—no instrument or price set. The enricher then posts this

Price onto the enricher-req-channel and waits for a reply. A service activator, which acts as the enricher listening on the enricher-req-channel, consumes the messages and enriches and returns the Price. The return value is published on the reply-channel. The enricher continues processing once it receives a message on the reply-channel. It adds the additional properties such as price and instrument to the message and sends them to the output-channel.

The following snippet shows the published Price. Note that the Price does not have any initial values set (they will be set via the PriceEnricher).

```
public void publishPrice() {
  //Create a Price object with no values
  Price p = new Price();

  // note the reply-channel as header property
  Message<Price> msg = MessageBuilder.withPayload(p)
    .setHeader(MessageHeaders.REPLY_CHANNEL, "reply-channel")
    .build();

  channel.send(msg, 10000);
  System.out.println("Price Message published.");
}
```

The PriceEnricher is given the message (via Service Activator) to enrich. We can use any complex logic here to set the data:

```
public class PriceEnricher {
  public Price enrichHeader(Message m) {
    Price p = (Price)m.getPayload();
    p.setInstrument("IBM");
    p.setPrice(111.11);
    return p;
  }
}
```

The Enricher component follows a Gateway pattern, which is discussed in the next section.

Gateway

If the prime requirement of your project is to write applications without requiring knowledge of the messaging system or connecting to a messaging framework, then the Gateway pattern is the one to use. We have previously seen some examples of sending and receiving messages by various publishers and consumers. However, we were fetching a reference to the channels from the application context every time we wanted to publish or consume a message. This means that our client code is tied to Framework's messaging components.

When you use the Gateway pattern, you will not be using any of the messaging components, but will be dealing with a simple interface that will expose your functionality.

Essentially, there are two types of Gateways: Synchronous Gateway and Asynchronous Gateway. In Synchronous Gateway, the message call will be blocked until the process is completed. In Asynchronous Gateway, the message call is not blocked. More on each gateway appears in their respective sections below.

Synchronous Gateway

The first step in writing a gateway is to define an interface that describes the interaction methods with the messaging system. In our example, we have an ITradeGateway interface with a single method processTrade. This is the only interface that will be exposed to the client with no implementation provided.

```
public interface ITradeGateway {
  public Trade processTrade(Trade t);
}
```

The next step is to configure a gateway:

```
<int:gateway id="tradeGateway"
  default-request-channel="trades-in-channel"
  default-reply-channel="trades-out-channel"
  service-interface="com.madhusudhan.jsi.endpoints.gateway.ITradeGateway" />
```

There's a lot happening in the backend.

When the application context is loaded with the above configuration, a gateway endpoint is created with default request and reply channels. The gateway has a service-interface attribute which points to our ITradeGateway interface. The framework's GatewayProxyFactoryBean creates a proxy for this service interface (and that's the reason you don't have to provide any implementation for the interface). The proxy will serve the client's incoming and outgoing requests using the channels provided.

So, if a client calls a processTrade method, it will be served by the proxy. It publishes a Message with a Trade object onto the trades-in-channel. The proxy then blocks the call until it receives a reply from the trades-out-channel. The reply is then passed back to the client. There will be another component picking up a message from the trades-in-channel to process the Trade accordingly.

The client code looks like this:

```
public GatewayEndpointTest() {
  ...
  public GatewayEndpointTest() {
    ctx = new ClassPathXmlApplicationContext("endpoints-gateway-beans.xml");
    // obtain our service interface
    tradeGateway = ctx.getBean("tradeGateway",ITradeGateway.class);
  }

  public void publishTrade(Trade t) {
    // call the method to publish the trade!
    Trade it = tradeGateway.processTrade(t);
    System.out.println("Trade Message published (Reply)."+it.getStatus());
  }
```

```
    public static void main(String[] args) {
      GatewayEndpointTest test = new GatewayEndpointTest();
      Trade t = new Trade();
      test.publishTrade(t);
    }
  }
```

We get the `tradeGateway` bean (which is the service interface) from the application context and invoke the `processTrade` method. There is no dependency on the messaging framework in this code. From the client's perspective, the client is invoking a method on a service interface.

To complete the example, we can configure a Service Activator to pick up messages from the `trades-in-channel` (this is the same channel where the messages are published by the proxy) and post the replies to the `trades-out-channel` (this is the same channel where the proxy is listening for replies). The following code snippet illustrates the Service Activator endpoint:

```
<int:service-activator
  input-channel="trades-in-channel"
  output-channel="trades-out-channel"
  ref="tradeProcessor"
  method="receiveTrade" >
</int:service-activator>

<bean id="tradeProcessor"
  class="com.madhusudhan.jsi.endpoints.gateway.TradeProcessor" />
```

The `TradeProcessor` is a simple class that is invoked by the `Activator` endpoint when a message arrives at the `trades-in-channel`. It then processes the Trade and sends a reply (via the return value):

```
public class TradeProcessor {
  public Trade receiveTrade(Trade t) {
    System.out.println("Received the Trade via Gateway:"+t);
    t.setStatus("PROCESSED");
    return t;
  }
}
```

Asynchronous Gateway

The client in the above example will be blocked until it gets a reply from the processors. If the client's requirement is to fire and continue, using Asynchronous Gateway is the right choice.

In order to achieve the asynchronous behavior, the service interface is required to have the return type changed so it now returns a `Future` object:

```
import java.util.concurrent.Future;

public interface ITradeGatewayAsync {
  public Future<Trade> processTrade(Trade t);
}
```

This is the only change required to make the gateway behave asynchronously. In your client program, the `processTrade` will now return a reply to your message as a `Future` object:

```
public void publishTrade(Trade t) {
  Future<Trade> f = tradeGateway.processTrade(t);
  try {
    Trade ft = f.get();
  } catch (Exception e) { .. }
}
```

Delayer

The `Delayer` endpoint is used to introduce delay between sender and receiver. This component forces the messages to be delivered at a later time based on the configuration. It will pick up a message from an input channel, apply the delay and send to the output channel when delay expires.

The configuration is simple, as demonstrated in the following snippet:

```
<int:delayer default-delay="5000"
  input-channel="in-channel"
  output-channel="out-channel">
</int:delayer>
```

All messages arriving at the `in-channel` will be delivered to the `out-channel` after a delay of five seconds. The messages will be delivered instantly if the `default-delay` is set to zero or negative.

You can also use a `header` field to define the delay period for each message. In order to do this, you need to let the framework know by using the attribute `delay-header-name` as shown below:

```
<int:delayer default-delay="5000"
  input-channel="prices-in-channel"
  output-channel="prices-out-channel"
  delay-header-name="MSG_DELAY">
</int:delayer>
```

All messages which have an `MSG_DELAY` header attribute will have a delay set by the value of the header field. Messages with no `MSG_DELAY` header attribute will have `default-delay` set on them.

Spring Expressions

Spring Integration endpoints support Spring Expression Language (SpEL) definitions. You can use the expressions to evaluate the properties on headers and payloads. For example, if you wish to extract a `header` property using the expression, the following snippet will help:

```
<int:header-enricher id="enricher"
  input-channel="in-channel" output-channel="out-channel">

  <int:header name="TARGET_SYSTEM" expression="headers.TARGET_SYSTEM"/>
</int:header-enricher>
```

The headers property will have the reference to MessageHeaders, so you can query the properties using headers.property_name syntax.

Similarly, the payload is available as the payload property, so you can query the payload object's variable by using dot notation:

```
<int:enricher input-channel="in-channel"
  request-channel="enricher-req-channel"
  output-channel="stdout">
  <int:property name="price"
    expression="payload.price"/>
</int:enricher>
```

Endpoints such as Transformers, Filters, Service Activators, and Splitters support the Spring Expressions.

Scripting Support

Spring Integration components can leverage Framework's extensive support for scripting languages. You can write scripts in your favorite Framework-supported language and invoke those scripts from its endpoints. In fact, you can use any scripting language that implements JSR-223 (*Scripting for Java Platform*). Some of the languages Framework supports are Groovy, Python/Jython, Ruby/JRuby, and JavaScript.

Let's take an example of a Transformer that calls a Groovy script for transformation. The endpoint picks up the message from the in-channel and passes it to the position-transformer.groovy script.

```
<int:transformer
  input-channel="in-channel"
  output-channel="stdout">
  <int-script:script lang="groovy"
    location="/home/mkonda/justspring/jsi/position-transformer.groovy"/>
</int:transformer>
```

The script will have access to the MessageHeaders and Payload of the Message in its execution context via headers and payload variables. You can also embed your script inline as CDATA in your config file.

For the Curious: Endpoint API

Now that you have seen the basic types of consumers, you should understand where they are really used. Under normal circumstances, you do not have to use them, as you will be configuring them under an XML namespace. The framework provides these components under various namespaces, so you can add the respective elements declaratively straight out of the box. This reduces the amount of coding and encourages a declarative programming model.

But for now, keep in mind that Transformers, Filters, Routers, etc., are all supported by the spring XML namespace. This means you can declaratively create an instance of any of these flow components. For example, a transformer element is used to create a Transformer component which will fetch messages from the input channel to kick off the transformation.

Understanding the link between the classes and namespace elements will give us much more command of the framework. *However, you are strongly encouraged to use namespaces to configure these endpoints, instead of using the API classes.*

Consumers

If you recall from the earlier chapter on channels, there are two types of channels: one is pollable while the other is subscribable. Based on the same definition, we have two types of endpoint consumers: *Polling Consumer* and an *Event-Driven Consumer*.

A PollingConsumer polls the channel for messages based on a polling configuration. It is driven by the client program. The EventDrivenConsumer, on the other hand, subscribes to a subscribable channel so it will be notified asynchronously when a message arrives at the channel.

Polling Consumers

One of the characteristics of polling consumers is to poll for messages in a timely fashion. Framework provides the PollingConsumer class that does this job. The class is instantiated by using a constructor that takes the reference to a pollable channel and a message handler. The message handler is a simple interface to handle the messages published onto the channel.

The following snippet shows how to create a PollingConsumer object. You can use the framework's class as is, or if preferred, create a wrapper around it.

```
private MessageHandler positionsHandler = null;
private QueueChannel positionsChannel = null;
...

// Instantiating a PollingConsumer
PollingConsumer consumer = new PollingConsumer(positionsChannel, positionsHandler);
```

Let's take an example of a custom consumer.

The PositionsPollingConsumer is a message consumer that grabs the Position messages from the positions-channel. We know that we can use the receive method on the channel itself to receive the message (shown in the following snippet), which has been described in earlier chapters.

```
Message m = channel.receive();//or other receive methods
System.out.println("Payload: " + m.getPayload());
```

Instead, what we do here is create an endpoint that polls from these channels. Channels merely act as buckets for messages, which is actually their main function.

As mentioned above, the `PollingConsumer` requires a channel and a handler to be instantiated. The handler is created by implementing the framework's `MessageHandler`:

```
public class PositionsHandler implements MessageHandler {
  public void handleMessage(Message<?> message) throws MessagingException {
    System.out.println("Handling a message: "+ message.getPayload().toString());
  }
}
```

The `PollingPositionsConsumer`, shown below, creates an instance of the framework's `PollingConsumer` to fetch the messages programmatically, rather than declaratively.

```
public class PositionsPollingConsumer {
  private PollingConsumer consumer = null;
  private PositionsHandler positionsHandler = null;

  public PositionsPollingConsumer(ApplicationContext ctx, QueueChannel
positionsChannel) {
    //instance of handler
    positionsHandler = new PositionsHandler();
    // now create the framework's consumer
    consumer = new PollingConsumer(positionsChannel, positionsHandler);
    //You must set the context, or else an error will be thrown
    consumer.setBeanFactory(ctx);
  }
  public void startConsumer() {
    consumer.start();
  }
}
```

Now that our consumer is coded, it's just a matter of calling the `startConsumer()` method. This method calls the `start` method on `PollingConsumer` internally:

```
PositionsPollingConsumer ppc = new PositionsPollingConsumer(ctx, positionsChannel);

ppc.startConsumer();
```

Polling Using Triggers. The `PollingConsumer` coded above does not poll—it just picks up the messages. However, we wish to add the function of polling to the component so it will poll in a timely fashion. This is achieved using the framework's Triggers.

There are two types of triggers provided by the framework: `PeriodicTrigger`, which polls at a fixed interval, and `CronTrigger`, which polls based on Unix's `cron` expressions. The `CronTrigger` is more flexible when the task scheduling has complex requirements.

Once an appropriate Trigger is chosen, it needs to be instantiated and wired onto the consumer. For example, if we want to poll every two seconds, create the `Peri odicTrigger` as shown below. You can also set other properties, such as `initialDelay` and `fixedRate`, to control the polling much further.

```
PeriodicTrigger periodicTrigger = new PeriodicTrigger(2000);
// let the polling kick in after half a second
periodicTrigger.setInitialDelay(500);
// fixed rate polling?
periodicTrigger.setFixedRate(false);
```

The `initialDelay` is set to start the polling only after the expiry of that time period. The `fixedRate` is a Boolean variable that will indicate if the polling should be done on a regular time interval. If, for whatever reason, the current message processing has taken more than the polling period (two seconds in the above example), the poller will poll for another message if this flag is set to `true`.

The `CronTrigger` enables the consumer to do more sophisticated polling. For example, you have a job that wakes up at midnight on weekdays to do house clean-up. It works on setting up `cron` expressions which can cater to such complex scenarios.

Cron expressions are expressed as space-separated fields. There are six such fields, each field representing an aspect of time. Declare an expression that represents your time requirements and pass it on to the `trigger` object as shown below:

```
// start polling all weekdays at exactly one minute past midnight
String cronExpression="* 01 00 * * MON-FRI";

cronTrigger = new CronTrigger(cronExpression);
```

The above `cron` expression allows the poller to wake one minute past midnight on all weekdays to check. The poller checks for any messages when it wakes, processes them, and goes back to sleep mode.

Event-Driven Consumers

The second type of endpoint consumers that subscribe rather than poll to the message stream is categorized as Event-Driven Consumers. The framework defines this type of consumer as an `EventDrivenConsumer` class. Their fundamental characteristic is that they wait for someone (the framework's responsibility) to deliver the message as soon as it appears on the channel. From our earlier discussions on event messages, you know that `SubscribableChannel` supports this type of consumer.

The instantiation of this consumer is exactly like that of `PollingConsumer`—supply a channel to which it should subscribe to get a message stream and a handler to handle the messages.

```
private EventDrivenConsumer consumer = null;
private PositionsHandler positionsHandler = null;
private ApplicationContext ctx = null;

public PositionsEventDrivenConsumer(ApplicationContext ctx,
  PublishSubscribeChannel positionsChannel) {

  positionsHandler = new PositionsHandler();

  // instantiate the event driven consumer
```

```
consumer = new EventDrivenConsumer(positionsChannel, positionsHandler);
consumer.setBeanFactory(ctx);
```

The PositionsHandler is a simple class that implements MessageHandler with providing the handleMessage method. Starting the consumer is as simple as calling the start method on the EventDrivenConsumer:

```
public void startConsumer() {
  // EventDrivenConsumer exposes start method
  consumer.start();
}
```

Unless you have a compelling requirement, use EventDrivenConsumer.

Summary

In this chapter, we discussed common endpoints such as Service Activator, Message Bridge, Enricher, Gateway, and Delayer. We touched on the workings of Spring Expressions and Scripting Support. We also looked at the fundamentals behind the endpoint consumers. We learned about PollingConsumer and EventDrivenConsumer receivers. We looked at ways of setting up the triggers on pollable channels in a more robust way.

CHAPTER 5

Transformers

Introduction

Not all applications understand the data they consume. Sometimes the messages need to be transformed before they can be consumed to achieve a business purpose. For example, a producer uses a Java Object as its payload to produce a message, while a consumer is interested in non-Java Object types like plain XML or name-value pairs.

To help the producer and consumer communicate, transformers are used to transform Java Object to non-Java Objects. The Spring Integration framework provides the transformer components that do exactly what is required. This chapter looks in detail at the transformation endpoints provided by the framework.

First, we will discuss the transformers like `Object-to-String` or `Object-to-Map` transformers, which come out of the box from the Spring Integration framework. We then discuss the ways to create our own transformers if the built-in ones are inadequate.

Built-In Transformers

Framework provides a couple of built-in transformers so you don't have to create them for simple cases such as converting an `Object` to `String`, `Map`, or `JSON` formats. The integration namespace supports these transformers.

String Transformers

Using the `Object to String` transformer is easy—all we have to do is define one in our bean's XML using the `object-to-string-transformer` element. The following snippet shows the definition:

```
<int:object-to-string-transformer
  input-channel="in-channel"
  output-channel="stdout">
</int:object-to-string-transformer>
```

```
<int-stream:stdout-channel-adapter id="stdout"/>
```

So, any POJOs (Plain Old Java Objects) appearing in the trades-in-channel will automatically be converted to string without intervention by custom transformers. Note
that we do not provide reference to any transformer in the above config definition. In
fact, the object-to-string-transformer element will not take the ref attribute. The
payload at the receiver's end will always be a toString() of the POJO. In the above
example, the payload is written to the stdout using the stdout-channel-adapter. So,
make sure your published POJO has overridden the toString() method, or else
you will see gibberish as your String payload (such as com.madhusud
han.jsi.domain.Trade@309ff0a8).

Map Transformers

If you need to convert the POJO to a name-value pair of Map, you can use the Object
to Map transformer. It is represented by the object-to-map-transformer element that
takes the payload from the input channel and emits a name-value paired Map object
onto the output channel.

```
<int:object-to-map-transformer
   input-channel="in-channel"
   output-channel="stdout">
</int:object-to-map-transformer>

<int-stream:stdout-channel-adapter id="stdout"/>
```

The above snippet's output is printed to the console using the stdout-channel-
adapter as below:

```
{direction=BUY, account=B12D45, security=null,
   status=NEW, quantity=0, id=1234}
```

Conversely, the map-to-object-transformer is used to convert the name-valued pairs
of Map to a Java Object. The use of the element is shown in the snippet below:

```
<int:map-to-object-transformer
   input-channel="in-channel"
   output-channel="stdout">
</int:map-to-object-transformer>
```

Serializing and Deserializing Transformers

Readers familiar with Java Message Service (JMS) will know that the messages must be
serialized and deserialized when sent or received, respectively. The Payload Serializ
ing transformer transforms a POJO to a byte array. It is represented below by payload-
serializing-transformer:

```
<int:payload-serializing-transformer
   input-channel="trades-in-channel"
   output-channel="trades-out-channel">
```

```
</int:payload-serializing-transformer>
```

When a `SerializableTrade` is published onto the `trades-in-channel`, the transformer picks and converts the payload to bytes. The deserializing transformer is then used to read the bytes back to `SerializableTrade`.

The deserializing transformer works in exactly the opposite manner as its counterpart by deserializing the serialized payload to a POJO message. It is represented by **payload-deserializing-transformer** and reads a byte array. The following snippet demonstrates a deserializing transformer printing out the `toString()` of `SerializableTrade` onto the console by picking up the bytes from the `trades-out-channel`, the output channel of the Serializing Transformer.

```
<int:payload-deserializing-transformer
   input-channel="trades-out-channel"
   output-channel="stdout">

</int:payload-deserializing-transformer>

<int-stream:stdout-channel-adapter id="stdout"/>
```

JSON Transformers

JavaScript Object Notation (JSON) is the lightweight message data exchange format that is completely language independent. It produces human-readable, formatted name values. The Spring Integration framework supports automatic transformations from an Object to JSON representation. As the name suggests, the `object-to-json-trans former` transforms an Object to JSON-formatted payload.

```
<int:object-to-json-transformer
   input-channel="trades-in-channel"
   output-channel="stdout">
</int:object-to-json-transformer>
```

Using our `Trade` object, the expected JSON format is printed to the console:

```
{"id":"1234","direction":"BUY","account":"B12D45","security":null,"status":
"NEW","quantity":0}
```

The `json-to-object-transformer` acts the other way—converting the JSON formatted payload to a Java Object. The `type` attribute specifies the type of object that the transformer needs to instantiate and populate with the input JSON data.

```
<int:json-to-object-transformer
   input-channel="trades-in-channel"
   output-channel="trades-out-channel"
   type="com.madhusudhan.jsi.domain.Trade">
</int:json-to-object-transformer>
```

XML Transformers

For those applications which use XML as the message format, the framework provides support in converting a POJO to XML and vice versa automatically. There's a bit more involved than simply using an XML tag, as we see in the above built-in transformers. If you have already worked with Spring's Object-to-XML (OXM) framework, this section will be easy.

Spring uses two classes to marshal and unmarshal the Object into XML and vice versa: the `org.springframework.oxm.Marshaller` and the `org.springframework.oxm.Unmarshaller`. The Marshaller is used to convert an Object to an XML Stream, while the Unmarshaller does the opposite—converting an XML stream to an Object.

You need to access the XML transformers using an XML namespace. The following highlighted code shows the importation of another namespace in our XML file:

```
<?xml version="1.0" encoding="UTF-8"?>

<beans xmlns="http://www.springframework.org/schema/beans"
    ...
    xmlns:int-xml="http://www.springframework.org/schema/integration/xml"

    xsi:schemaLocation="http://www.springframework.org/schema/beans
    ....
    http://www.springframework.org/schema/integration/xml
    http://www.springframework.org/schema/integration/xml/
    spring-integration-xml-2.1.xsd">
</beans>
```

Once you declare the namespaces, use the `marshalling-transformer` element to read a message off an input channel. The message is formatted into XML and posted back to the output channel. See the wiring of the `marshalling-transformer` below:

```
<int-xml:marshalling-transformer
    input-channel="trades-in-channel"
    output-channel="stdout"
    marshaller="marshaller"
    result-type="StringResult">

</int-xml:marshalling-transformer>

<bean id="marshaller"
  class="org.springframework.oxm.castor.CastorMarshaller" />
```

As expected, the `marshalling-transformer` picks up the messages from an input channel and spits out an XML-formatted message onto a standard output. The noteworthy point is the wiring of the `marshaller` and the `result-type`. The referenced marshaler is a `CastorMarshaller` which is declared as a bean in the same `config` file.

The output of the message is printed below (note that I've formatted the output result with new lines for clarity):

```
Payload:
<?xml version="1.0" encoding="UTF-8"?>
<trade>
  <status>NEW</status>
  <account>B12D45</account>
  <direction>BUY</direction>
  <id>1234</id>
</trade>
```

The marshalling-transformer takes an optional result-type which decides the result type. There are two built-in result types—javax.xml.transform.dom.DOMResult and org.springframework.xml.transform.StringResult. The DOMResult is the default one, meaning if you don't provide the result-type, the output message payload will be of the DOMResult type.

If you wish to use your own custom result-type transformer, you have the option of providing a result-factory attribute.

```
<int-xml:marshalling-transformer
    input-channel="trades-in-channel-xml"
    output-channel="trades-out-channel-xml"
    marshaller="marshaller"
    result-factory="tradeResultFactory">
</int-xml:marshalling-transformer>

<bean id="tradeResultFactory"
class="com.madhusudhan.jsi.transformers.builtin.TradeResultFactory" />
```

The TradeResultFactory has one method to implement—createResult, inherited from ResultFactory:

```
public class TradeResultFactory implements ResultFactory {

  public Result createResult(Object payload) {

    System.out.println("Creating result ->"+payload);
    //create your own implementation of Result
    return new TradeResult();
  }
}
```

XPath Transformers

The xpath-transformer decodes the XML payload using XPath expressions. The transformer expects an XML payload on an input channel and outputs the result to the output channel after applying the XPath expression. The configuration is simple:

```
<int-xml:xpath-transformer
  input-channel="trades-in-channel"
  output-channel="stdout"
  xpath-expression="/trade/@status">

<int:poller fixed-rate="1000" />
</int-xml:xpath-transformer>
```

Create and publish the XML payload message as shown below onto the **trades-in-**
channel:

```
private String createNewTradeXml() {
  return "<trade status='NEW' account='B12D45' direction='BUY'/>";
}
```

The input message's payload will be parsed for a status attribute's value and will print
it to the console:

```
//publishes the status onto stdout:
```

```
NEW
```

Custom Transformers

Now that we have seen out-of-the-box transformers, it is time to see how we can create
our own Transformers should the need arise.

Let us look at an example of a `TradePublisher` that will produce `Trade` messages with a
`Trade` POJO as a payload. In the example, the consumer is not interested in receiving
a Java Object but is expecting a name-value paired map. Can we tweak the
`TradePublisher` to produce the Trade data compatible with that of a receiver? Yes, we
can, but what if we have another receiver that may come up a few weeks later and be
interested in consuming XML-formatted `Trade` messages?

Ideally, the producers should be unaware of consumers or their requirements. They
only talk via an intermediary called `message`. This enables the applications to be decoupled, too. Our `TradePublisher` produces the Trades in a universal format—a POJO.

Before the message hits the receiver, a transformer needs to be plugged in.

Trade Map Transformer

Because the receiver is expecting name-value pairs of the Trade data, we need to transform the message into the expected format before sending to the consumer. One way
to do this is to create a class that transforms the POJO to a name-value pair. The
`TradeMapTransformer` class defined below satisfies this requirement:

```
public class TradeMapTransformer {
  public Map<String, String> transform(Trade t) {
    Map<String,String> tradeNameValuesMap = new HashMap<String,String>();

    tradeNameValuesMap.put("TRADE_ID", t.getId());
    tradeNameValuesMap.put("TRADE_ACCOUNT", t.getAccount());
    ...
    return tradeNameValuesMap;
  }
}
```

As you can see, the `TradeMapTransformer` is a simple class that takes the `Trade` object and creates a map of values.

Now that we have the transformer, we need to let the framework know that it should use our class when a message appears on the input channel. The way to do this is to declare the `transformer` element in your beans file and, via this element, glue the endpoint to the channel:

```
<int:transformer input-channel="trades-in-channel"
  output-channel="trades-out-channel" ref="tradeMapTransformer">
</int:transformer>

<bean id="tradeMapTransformer"
  class="com.madhusudhan.jsi.transformers.custom.TradeMapTransformer" />
```

You need to define these few bits when declaring the `transformer` element: an input channel, an output channel, and of course, a transformer implementor. In the above configuration, the transformer picks up a message that appears in the `trades-in-chan nel`, transforms it into name-values, and publishes it back to the output channel, `trades-out-channel` in this case, as a `Map` of name-values. The `ref` attribute refers to our transformer class, `TradeMapTransformer` in this instance.

Once the message is received from the channel, the payload is extracted from it. Under normal circumstances, the payload will be whatever the publisher has sent. However, we have a transformer between the publisher and the consumer that transforms the message from the POJO format to the name-value format. Hence, the payload will be of the type returned by the `transform` method.

In the above case, our `TradeMapTransformer` returns a `Map<String,String>`—hence the `getPayload()` method is casted to a `Map`.

The output of the program invokes `toString()` on the `Map` object to produce the following to the console:

```
Payload: {TRADE_DIRECTION=BUY, TRADE_ACCOUNT=B12D45, TRADE_ID=1234,
TRADE_STATUS=NEW, TRADE_SECURITY=null}
...
Payload: {TRADE_DIRECTION=BUY, TRADE_ACCOUNT=B12D45, TRADE_ID=1234,
TRADE_STATUS=NEW, TRADE_SECURITY=null}
```

String Transformer

The above `TradeMapTransformer` cannot be used if there's a requirement to consume Trades in a `String` format. There's a simple solution to this—create a *POJO-to-String* Transformer. The following snippet shows how the transformer converts a `Trade` object to a `String`:

```
public class PojoToStringTransformer {
  private final String tradeString
    = "TRADE_ID=%s,
       TRADE_ACCOUNT=%s,
```

```
            TRADE_SECURITY=%s,
            TRADE_DIRECTION=%s,
            TRADE_STATUS=%s" ;

    public String transform ( Trade t ) {
      return
        String.format(  tradeString,
                        t.getId(),
                        t.getAccount(),
                        t.getSecurity(),
                        t.getDirection(),
                        t.getStatus() ) ;
    }
}
```

Next, we connect this transformer into our configuration:

```
<int:transformer input-channel="trades-in-channel"
    output-channel="trades-out-channel"
    ref="pojoToStringTransformer">
</int:transformer>

<bean id="pojoToStringTransformer"
  class="com.madhusudhan.jsi.transformers.custom.PojoToStringTransformer" />
```

The output of the executed program prints the following:

```
Payload: TRADE_ID=1234,TRADE_ACCOUNT=B12D45,TRADE_SECURITY=null,
TRADE_DIRECTION=BUY,TRADE_STATUS=NEW
...
Payload: TRADE_ID=1234,TRADE_ACCOUNT=B12D45,TRADE_SECURITY=null,
TRADE_DIRECTION=BUY,TRADE_STATUS=NEW
```

The above shows that it is easy to plug in transformers. It will also save time on writing code when all you have to do is declare a transformer element and set a few properties.

Using Annotations

You can use Framework's `@Transformer` annotation to refer to the transformer bean from your `config` file. The `component-scan` allows the container to scan for annotated beans in the `transformers` package, In this case, the `AnnotatedTradeMapTransformer` class will be instantiated:

```
@Component
public class AnnotatedTradeMapTransformer {
  @Transformer
  public Map<String, String> transform(Trade t) {
    Map<String,String> tradeNameValuesMap =
      new HashMap<String,String>();
    ....
    return tradeNameValuesMap;
  }
}
```

The annotated `transform` method is invoked when a message arrives in the in-channel. The configuration is similar to the one we have already seen, except the `component-scan` tag is added. This scans for the beans decorated with `@Component` and creates instances of them once found in the application context container:

```
<context:component-scan
  base-package="com.madhusudhan.jsi.flow.transformer" />
```

Summary

Transformers play an important role in satisfying different clients' requirements. They form a vital part of creating seamless integration between the endpoints. In this chapter, we discussed the workings of Transformers in detail. We touched on various aspects of Transformers, including the difference between the custom and built-in transformers. Finally, we explored the transformers used for transforming real word objects to XML and vice versa.

In the next chapter, Chapter 6, we will discuss message flow components, such as Filters, Routers, Aggregators, and Splitters.

Flow Components

Introduction

Messaging applications sometimes require additional components like routing, aggregation, or sequencing. An application might have specific criteria to route messages to multiple channels or to split the messages and later aggregate them for further processing.

Spring Integration includes these requirements and supports them with message flow components that include Filters, Routers, Aggregators, and Splitters. These components do not require extra coding and can be used as is out of the box.

This chapter will discuss each of these components in detail.

Filters

Consumers have different message requirements, with some wanting one type of message and others wanting a different type. Spring Integration Framework uses *Filters* and sets up criteria to decide which applications should receive the messages and which should not.

Let's look at an example of Trades being published onto a `trades-in-channel`, which is configured to receive all types of Trades published by producers.

This requirement can be fulfilled in two ways without using Framework.

- Create and configure `NewTradeConsumer` to only pick up messages with `trade Type=NEW` and throw away everything else, and create and configure `Cancel TradeReceiver` to only consume Trades with `tradeType=CANCEL`.

- Have a single receiver (e.g., `TradeConsumer`) that consumes all incoming messages regardless of the type of Trade, which then invokes the appropriate processing component based on the Trade type (e.g., by using `if-else`).

Although these two methods work fine, they are not ideal.

In both cases, most of the filtering work is done by the consumers. What happens if we have to introduce another set of filtering conditions?

As filtering is a common task, Spring Integration's Filters can be configured to do this task and leave the consumers to receive their choice of messages. The framework takes away the filtering logic from the applications and ties it in with the channels.

Using Custom Filters

Framework provides a `filter` namespace for declaring the filters in configuration files. The `filter` element has an input channel to read the input messages, an output channel to deliver the accepted messages, and a reference to the filter bean. In the example below, the filter bean is a simple class that has the logic of accepting only NEW Trades:

```
<int:filter input-channel="in-channel"
            output-channel="out-channel"
            ref="newTradeFilter"
            method="isNewTrade">
</int:filter>

<bean id="newTradeFilter" class="com.madhusudhan.jsi.flow.ex1.NewTradeFilter" />
```

The rejected messages (non NEW Trades) are filtered out immediately and thrown away by the framework. The `method` attribute indicates the method to be called on the New TradeFilter class when a message is picked up by this endpoint. The only mandatory requirement is that it must return a Boolean value. In this way, the framework can either accept or discard the message.

The following is the implementation of the class:

```
public class NewTradeFilter {

  public boolean isNewTrade(Message<?> message) {
    Trade t = (Trade)message.getPayload();
    return (t.getStatus().equalsIgnoreCase("new"));
  }
}
```

The `isNewTrade` method accepts a `Trade` message and checks the status by calling get Status() on the object. If the status is NEW, the method returns `true`, which means that the `Message` is passed onto the next component, or else discarded.

You can omit declaring the `method` attribute from the filter configuration if your class has just one method defined. Framework is intelligent enough to pick up the defined single method.

There are advantages to using your own custom filters. One advantage is that you are not tied to the framework. A bigger advantage is that you might have one filter class catering all of your universal filtering logic.

Using Framework's MessageSelector

You can also create Filters by implementing Framework's `MessageSelector` to create a filter bean. One mandatory requirement is to expose the `accept` method. This method returns a Boolean value—if true, the message is sent to the channel, or else the message is not forwarded. It is your logic in the `accept` method that does the filtering of criteria.

The following snippet is an example of the `CancelTradeFilter` implementing the `MessageSelector` interface:

```
public class CancelTradeFilter implements MessageSelector{
  public boolean accept(Message<?> message) {
    Trade t = (Trade)message.getPayload();
    return (t.getStatus().equalsIgnoreCase("cancel"));
  }
}
```

The `accept` method checks every message to see if the Trade's status is `CANCEL`. Wiring the filter follows the same principle:

```
<int:filter input-channel="in-channel"
            output-channel="out-channel"
            ref="cancelTradeFilter">
</int:filter>

<bean id="cancelTradeFilter"
class="com.madhusudhan.jsi.flow.filters.CancelTradeFilter" />
```

In both cases, we have defined the custom filter bean using the `ref` attribute outside the filter so it can be reused if required. However, you can also declare the filter as an inner bean:

```
<int:filter input-channel="in-channel"
            output-channel="out-channel">
  <!-- Inner Bean -->
  <bean class="com.madhusudhan.jsi.flow.filters.NewTradeFilter" />
</int:filter>
```

The `ref` attribute is not required, as we have declared the filter bean inline. Note that, because the filter is defined as an inner bean, other beans in the same application context will not have access to this filter.

Using Annotations

Another way—simple and straightforward—of creating Filters is via Annotations. Here's an annotated version of `NewTradeFilter`:

```
@Component
public class AnnotatedNewTradeFilter {
```

```
@Filter
  public boolean isTradeCancelled(Message<?> message) {
    Trade t = (Trade)message.getPayload();
    return (t.getStatus().equalsIgnoreCase("cancel"));
  }

}
```

The framework uses the `@Filter` annotation to annotate the `isTradeCancelled` method shown above. The following snippet shows how the filter is configured:

```
<context:component-scan base-package="com.madhusudhan.jsi.flow.filter"/>

<int:filter input-channel="in-channel"
  output-channel="stdout"
  ref="annotatedNewTradeFilter" >
</int:filter>
```

The `component-scan` lets the container scan for annotated beans in the `filter` package, in this case, the `AnnotatedNewTradeFilter` class. The annotated method `isTradeCancelled` is invoked whenever an expected message arrives in the `in-channel`.

Discarded Messages

The filters will either accept a message or silently discard it. However, instead of discarding unwanted messages, you may want to log them for further analysis. Ideally, such messages should be quarantined for someone (e.g., a support team) to analyze. The framework allows the filter to raise an exception or forward it to another channel when the message doesn't fit the filter criteria.

To raise an exception, add the `throw-exception-on-rejection` attribute to the filter element. This is shown as highlighted code in the following snippet:

```
<int:filter input-channel="all-trades-in-channel"
            output-channel="cancel-trades-out-channel"
            ref="cancelTradeFilter"
            throw-exception-on-rejection="true">
</int:filter>
```

Alternatively, wire a channel into the `filter` element to receive the discarded messages. Use the `discard-channel` attribute to set the discarded channel.

```
<int:filter input-channel="all-trades-in-channel"
            output-channel="cancel-trades-out-channel"
            ref="cancelTradeFilter"
            discard-channel="non-cancel-trades-hospital-channel">
</int:filter>
```

You can then have a housekeeping task that regularly inspects the failed Trades appearing in this quarantine channel. If the message is treated, the message can be replayed back to the `Trades` channel.

Routers

One of the flow requirements is to send the messages to one or more channels based on certain criteria. A router component can be used to distribute the messages to multiple destinations. For example, the requirement is that all new Trades should be sent to `new-trades-in-channel` while all amended Trades are sent to `amended-trades-in-channel`. The `Router` component will take care of this task. The router picks up the message from a channel and redelivers (routes) it to the relevant channel based on `payload` or `headers` content.

There is a difference between the filters and routers. While Filter decides whether or not the message is to be sent based on a simple Boolean test, Router forwards the message to one or more channels based on content. There are only two options for a message that's being passed through a Filter—forwarded or discarded. If a filter is used, a message may or may not appear in an output channel, whereas if a router is used, a single message can be sent to one or more channels.

The framework provides a couple of built-in routers: `PayloadTypeRouter`, based on `payload` content, or `HeaderValueRouter`, based on `header` values.

PayloadTypeRouter

The `PayloadTypeRouter` determines the routing of messages to different channels based on the *type* of the `payload`. The router endpoint attached to an incoming channel will evaluate the type and accordingly distribute (route) the messages to other channels expecting that particular type. The `payload-type-router` element is used to plug in this type of routing logic.

For example, you have a channel where `Account` and `Trade` messages are flowing in from an external system, and you wish to separate them into two different channels. `Accounts` should go to `accounts-channel`, while `Trades` should go to `trades-channel`.

In order to achieve this, wire in a `payload-type-router` to the incoming channel, the `all-in-channel` which receives all types of messages. Next, use the `mapping` attribute to set the expected type and its corresponding channel. See below for the definition of this router:

```
<int:payload-type-router input-channel="all-in-channel">
  <int:mapping type="com.madhusudhan.jsi.flow.router.Trade"
    channel="trades-channel" />
  <int:mapping type="com.madhusudhan.jsi.flow.router.Account"
    channel="accounts-channel" />
</int:payload-type-router>
```

All the messages whose payload type is a Trade will be sent to `trades-channel`, while those of the `Account` type are sent to `accounts-out-channel`. It is a simple categorization based on payload type.

HeaderValueRouter

HeaderValueRouter deduces routing logic from the message header's properties. We define the logic by picking up a header property using the header-name attribute, as in the following declaration:

```
<int:header-value-router input-channel="all-in-channel"
                         header-name="status"
                         default-output-channel="no-matches-channel">
  <int:mapping value="NEW" channel="new-trades-channel" />
  <int:mapping value="CANCEL" channel="cancel-trades-channel" />
</int:header-value-router>
```

This is what happens: each message is checked against the incoming message's header property called status. If the status equals NEW, the message is pushed into new-trades-channel. If it matches CANCEL, it is published to cancel-trades-channel.

Custom Routers

We can use implementations to write our own custom logic for routing messages. To do so, we need to define a class that expects a message, parses the message (or header), and accordingly returns the channel name. The BigTradeRouter shown below implements a routing logic to forward any big Trades (whose quantity is greater than one million pounds) to a big-trades-channel.

```
public class BigTradeRouter {
  public String bigTrade(Message<Trade> message){
    Trade t = message.getPayload();

    // check if the trade is a big one and if it is
    // send it to a separate channel to handle them
    if(t.getQuantity() > 1000000)
      return "big-trades-channel";
    // else send a normal channel
    return "normal-trades-channel";
  }
}
```

Now that you have the router logic defined in your class, the next step is to wire it into the config file:

```
<int:router input-channel="all-in-channel"
  ref="bigTradeRouter"
  method="bigTrade"
  default-output-channel="non-matches-channel"/>

<!-- The custom router -->
<bean id="bigTradeRouter" class="com.madhusudhan.jsi.flow.router.BigTradeRouter"/>
```

As you can see, there is no mapping declared in the router element. Any message coming into the all-in-channel will be sent to BigTradeRouter to check if any of them is a big

Trade. If the condition is satisfied, the message is pushed into `big-trades-channel`, or else to `normal-trades-channel`, as coded in the class.

Recipient List Router

Another type of router available out of the box is a statistically defined recipient's list: a message to channels defined in a recipient's list.

The following snippet demonstrates a `Trade` message being distributed to three downstream channels—`persistor-channel` to persist all incoming Trades, `trades-channel` for processing the Trades, and `audit-channel` for auditing purposes.

The router is set up using the `recipient-list-router` element in integration namespace.

```
<int:recipient-list-router input-channel="all-in-channel">
  <int:recipient channel="persistor-channel"/>
  <int:recipient channel="trades-channel"/>
  <int:recipient channel="audit-channel"/>
</int:recipient-list-router>
```

Unqualified Messages

What happens to those messages that, for any reason, are not passed through the specified routing logic? The framework can either throw an exception or push them to a default channel. There's a `default-output-channel` present in the router elements which is used to publish routing logic for unqualified messages.

```
<int:payload-type-router
  input-channel="all-in-channel"
  default-output-channel="non-matches-channel">
  ...
</int:payload-type-router>
```

A `resolution-required` attribute set on the router acts in conjunction with the default output channel. The property will try to resolve any `MessageChannel` based on the channel ID. If the `resolution-required` is set to `true` but a `default-output-channel` cannot be resolved, an exception is thrown.

Routers Using Annotations

We can also create Routers using Framework's `@Router` annotation. All we have to do is decorate the appropriate method with this annotation on modified `Annotated BigTradeRouter` as shown below.

```
@Component
public class AnnotatedBigTradeRouter {
  @Router
  public String bigTrade(Message<Trade> message) {
    Trade t = message.getPayload();
```

```
      if (t.getQuantity() > 10000)
        return "big-trades-channel";
      return "trades-stdout";
    }
  }
```

You have to wire the above bean using the `ref` attribute in the configuration file:

```
<context:component-scan
  base-package="com.madhusudhan.jsi.flow.router" />

<int:router id="annonatedRouter" input-channel="in-channel"
  default-output-channel="no-matches-channel"
  ref="annotatedBigTradeRouter">
</int:router>
```

Note that the return value of the above `bigTrade` method returns a `String` value of the channel name. The return value can also return a solo `MessageChannel` or list of `MessageChannel` references.

Splitters

Splitters are used to split a message into pieces. The message will be dissected into smaller ones by custom logic for various consumers to act on. There are several scenarios for using splitters, such as splitting a large payload into smaller chunks or introducing parallel processing. The Spring Integration framework provides a `splitter` element into the `integration` namespace. The element will then refer to a splitter bean which implements the splitting logic.

You can implement `splitter` in various ways: you can either implement your own POJO with custom logic or extend Framework's `AbstractMessageSplitter` abstract class to implement the `splitMessage()` method. You can also use Annotations to define one.

Using Custom Splitters

If you choose to use custom splitters, all you have to do is create a simple POJO that implements the splitting algorithm.

Let's take an example of an incoming message consisting of a normal Trade and some encrypted data. The requirement is to extract this encrypted message into a different object, `EncryptedTrade`. The newly created `EncryptedTrade` and the old (original) Trade will be sent out to the output channel. The output channel will receive two messages, one which is a normal Trade with no encrypted message and a second message with the encrypted message represented by `EncryptedTrade` object. The preferred way to do this is to introduce a splitter component to split the incoming message into two Trades.

`Trade` and `EncryptedTrade` both inherit from `ITrade`, which is a marker interface (no methods).

The Trade object is an ITrade type object, which has a section to carry encryptedMessage, but at this stage it's in a String format.

```
public class Trade implements ITrade{
  private String encryptedMsg = null;
  ...

  public String getEncryptedMsg() {
    return encryptedMsg;
  }
  public void setEncryptedMsg(String encryptedMsg) {
    this.encryptedMsg = encryptedMsg;
  }
  ...
}
```

The EncryptedTrade is an ITrade type object carrying an encrypted message.

```
public class EncryptedTrade implements ITrade{

  private String encryptedMsg = null;

  public EncryptedTrade(String encryptedMsg) {
    this.encryptedMsg = encryptedMsg;
  }

  public String getEncryptedMsg() { ... }

  public void setEncryptedMsg(String encryptedMsg) { ... }
}
```

The idea is to extract the encryptedMessage string from a Trade object and construct an EncryptedMessage (the constructor of the EncryptedMessage takes a string) object. This is a split logic algorithm. The CustomEncryptedTradeSplitter shown below encapsulates this logic:

```
public class CustomEncryptedTradeSplitter{

  public List<ITrade> splitMyMessageToTrades(Message<?> message) {
    List<ITrade> trades = new ArrayList<ITrade>();
    TradeImpl t = (TradeImpl)message.getPayload();

    //Create a new object from the payload
    EncryptedTrade et = new EncryptedTrade(t.getEncryptedMsg());
    trades.add(t);
    trades.add(et);
    System.out.println("Splitting message done, list: "+trades);
    return trades;
  }
}
```

Now that you have the splitter bean ready, you use the ref attribute to wire it into the configuration. In addition, you should also mention the name of the method that should be invoked when splitting a message.

```
<!-- Custom splitter -->
<int:splitter input-channel="all-in-channel"
  ref="customEncryptedMessageSplitter"
  method="splitMyMessageToTrades"
  output-channel="all-trades-out-channel">
</int:splitter>

<bean id="customEncryptedMessageSplitter"
  class="com.madhusudhan.jsi.flow.splitter.CustomEncryptedTradeSplitter" />
```

Using AbstractMessageSplitter

Framework provides an abstract class that needs to be extended if you intend to go this route. The class is `AbstractMessageSplitter` and the method to implement is `splitMessage(Message<?> message)`. The modified `EncryptedTradeSplitter` extending the `AbstractMessageSplitter` is shown below:

```
public class EncryptedTradeSplitter extends AbstractMessageSplitter{
  @Override
  protected Object splitMessage(Message<?> message) {
    ....
    return trades;
  }

}
```

Once a message is received (remember the payload of this message is an `ITrade` object with `encryptedMessage` set) from the input channel, it is passed on to the `EncryptedTradeSplitter` instance. The `EncryptedTrade` is constructed using the incoming Trade's encrypted message. The `EncryptedTrade` and `Trade` are then added to a list and passed back.

Framework has now received a list of `ITrades` after calling the splitter. These two Trades are then published onto the `out-channel` specified in the wiring configuration.

```
<int:splitter input-channel="in-channel"
  ref="encryptedMessageSplitter"
  output-channel="out-channel">
</int:splitter>

<bean id="encryptedMessageSplitter"
  class="com.madhusudhan.jsi.flow.splitter.EncryptedTradeSplitter" />
```

The `ref` attribute specifies the splitter bean for implementing the splitting algorithm.

Using Annotations

You can also use the `@Splitter` annotation to let the framework know about your annotated splitter bean. You should decorate the method with the `@Splitter` annotation as shown in the following example:

```
@Component
public class AnnonatedEncryptedTradeSplitter{

    @Splitter
    public List<ITrade> splitMyMessageToTrades(Message<?> message) {
      ..
    }
}
```

The method returns a collection of objects, each of them wrapped in a Message as payload.

Splitter in the Background

We know that the splitter slices the parent message into many messages depending on our split logic. These child messages end up in the output channel. When working with Splitters, there are various things Framework does in the background:

- Stamping with the *same* CORRELATION_ID on each of the child messages
- Setting a property SEQUENCE_SIZE to the number of messages the parent was split into
- Stamping each message with a simple SEQUENCE_NUMBER

In order to understand these properties, let's take the earlier example of the splitter. The following is the output to the console by the receiver. It shows that it has received both messages.

```
Received a message:[Payload=Trade [...]][Headers={sequenceNumber=1,
    correlationId=18c9eee1-4795-4378-b70e-d236027d0c30, ..., sequenceSize=2}]

Received a message:[Payload=EncryptedTrade[...]][Headers={sequenceNumber=2,
    correlationId=18c9eee1-4795-4378-b70e-d236027d0c30, ..., sequenceSize=2}]
```

There are three interesting attributes to note in the above output:

1. The correlationId (represented by CORRELATION_ID header property) is the same for both messages so that these two message are correlated (children).
2. The sequenceSize attribute represented by the SEQUENCE_SIZE header property will indicate the number of messages that were formed out of one parent message. In the current example, the parent message has been split into two individual messages (sequenceSize=2).
3. The sequence number is represented by sequenceNumber on the message header. In the above output, the sequence number increases by one.

These three attributes are important when you attempt to reassemble the parent message. This is what an Aggregator does, as explained in the next section.

Aggregators

The job of Aggregators is to assemble multiple messages to create a single parent message. They are the opposite of splitters, since they require information to begin and end a task. They have to maintain state for this reason. They also need to follow certain strategies to correlate the messages and release them after they are aggregated.

This is a complex task because all the messages of a set have to arrive before the aggregators can start work. Before we look at a complicated aggregation task, let's consider a simple task based on default correlation and release strategies.

The TradeAggregator defined below is a simple aggregator whose job is to aggregate the incoming child Trades into a parent Trade.

```
public class TradeAggregator {

  public ITrade aggregateTrade(List<ITrade> childTrades) {
    ...
  }
}
```

This aggregator is declared using the following metadata:

```
<int:aggregator input-channel="in-channel"
                output-channel="agg-channel"
                ref="tradeAggregator"
                method="aggregateTrade">
</int:aggregator>

<bean id="tradeAggregator"
  class="com.madhusudhan.jsi.flow.aggregator.TradeAggregator" />

<!-- Splitter that would cut the messages for aggregator to re-build -->
<int:splitter input-channel="in-channel" ref="customSplitter"
  output-channel="out-channel">
  </int:splitter>
 <bean id="customSplitter"
   class="com.madhusudhan.jsi.flow.splitter.CustomEncryptedTradeSplitter" />
```

The ref and method attributes define a specific method on the POJO to be invoked whenever the release strategy is fulfilled. If the method is undefined, then the default release and correlation strategies are applied, as in the above case.

A splitter is added to the configuration so the incoming Trade is split into two child Trades and sent to the aggregator for rebuilding.

Strategies

The Aggregators do not work in isolation. They are paired with a couple of algorithms called strategies, which are very important for the way aggregators behave.

Let's take a case where a parent message is sliced (using a splitter) into a large number of child messages. The downstream aggregator needs to wait for these messages to arrive before it can produce the parent message again. It is the responsibility of the Aggregator to wait for all the messages to arrive before it begins its work, hence the complexity of its task.

There are certain algorithms that an aggregator follows in order to begin or end its work. These algorithms are provided to the aggregators as the *correlation* and *release* strategies.

The way to keep track of the influx of messages and aggregate them is by employing these strategies.

Correlation Strategy

This strategy defines the key for the grouping of the messages. The default grouping is based on the `CORRELATION_ID` message. Thus, all the messages with the same `CORRELATION_ID` will be stored in a separate bucket for aggregation.

The framework provides a `HeaderAttributeCorrelationStrategy` out of the box. You can also implement your own strategy, either by implementing the `CorrelationStrategy` interface or creating your own POJO. In the former case, you have to implement the `getCorrelationKey()` method that will return the key as shown below:

```
public class MyCorrelationStrategy implements CorrelationStrategy {

    public Object getCorrelationKey(Message<?> message) {
    // implement your own correlation key here
    // return ..
    }
}
```

Wire this strategy into your configuration using the `correlation-strategy` attribute:

```
<int:aggregator input-channel="all-trades-out-channel"
                output-channel="agg-channel"
                ref="tradeAggregator"
                method="aggregateTrade"
                correlation-strategy="myCorrelationStrategy">
</int:aggregator>

<bean id="myCorrelationStrategy"
    class="com.madhusudhan.jsi.flow.aggregator.MyCorrelationStrategy" />
```

If you do not wish to implement a `CorrelationStrategy` but have your own class (a POJO, for instance), then you have to identify the method name in the metadata definition:

```
<int:aggregator input-channel="all-trades-out-channel"
    ...
    correlation-strategy="myCorrelationStrategy"
```

```
                    correlation-strategy-method="fetchCorrelationKey">
     </int:aggregator>
```

The only requirement is that your aggregator's method should expect a `Message<?>` and
return an `Object`.

Release Strategy

The release strategy of an aggregator dictates at which point the collected messages
should be sent or released for aggregation. Until and unless the signal is sent, the
framework stores the messages, except when a `release-on-expire` flag is set.

The default strategy is represented by `SequenceSizeReleaseStrategy`, which implements
a `ReleaseStrategy` interface. It works on the algorithm that checks the presence of
messages grouped by `SEQUENCE_SIZE`. For example, if the `SEQUENCE_SIZE` is 10, the
strategy will trigger a signal to the aggregator to begin only after it receives all 10 messages with sequence numbers ranging from 1 to 10.

Similar to `CorrelationStrategy`, you can either implement the framework's
`ReleaseStrategy` or create your own custom class that can signal the release. The following code implements Framework's interface:

```java
public class MyReleaseStrategy implements ReleaseStrategy {
  public boolean canRelease(MessageGroup group) {
    // implement your strategy here
    return false;
  }
}
```

The final step is to wire the strategy to the aggregator element:

```
<int:aggregator input-channel="in-channel"
                output-channel="agg-channel"
                ref="tradeAggregator" method="aggregateTrade"
                correlation-strategy="myCorrelationStrategy"
                correlation-strategy-method="fetchCorrelationKey"
                release-strategy="myReleaseStrategy">
</int:aggregator>

<bean id="myReleaseStrategy"
  class="com.madhusudhan.jsi.flow.aggregator.MyReleaseStrategy" />
```

If you write your own implementation without locking into Framework's API, then the
method should expect a `java.util.List` Object returning a Boolean value. You need
to wire the bean using the `release-strategy` and `release-strategy-method` attributes:

```
<int:aggregator input-channel="in-channel"
                ...
                release-strategy="myReleaseStrategy"
                release-strategy-method="signalRelease">
</int:aggregator>
```

Message Store

Aggregators hold onto the messages until all of them have arrived. The messages cannot be released for aggregation if even one has not arrived (unless you set an expiry on the storage time). This means that having a place to store the messages is important for the aggregators to work.

The framework provides an option for setting a message store on aggregators. This store is used to keep the flowing messages grouped until a release signal or expiry time occurs.

There are two storage options: in-memory or external database.

The in-memory is the default storage which uses a simple `java.util.Map` to collect the messages in the application's memory. As an application's memory may be limited, care should be taken if this facility is used to store messages. Messages can also be lost if they are not backed up to a durable storage area in case the application crashes.

The second option is to use a database. The external location of the database should protect any loss of messages if the application crashes.

The framework provides a `message-store` attribute to refer to an appropriate message store. However, if the default message store is an in-memory one, you do not have to declare this attribute at all.

Should you wish to wire in a database store, use the following:

```
<int:aggregator input-channel="all-trades-out-channel"
                output-channel="agg-channel"
                ....
                message-store="mySqlStore">
</int:aggregator>

<bean id="mySqlStore" class="org.springframework.integration.jdbc.JdbcMessageStore">
  <property name="dataSource" ref="mySqlDataSource"/>
</bean>
```

The `mySqlStore` refers to Framework's `JdbcMessageStore`, to which a database should be wired.

Resequencers

An important characteristic of a messaging system is the order of the messages. Although in some cases, the ordering defeats the performance, it is sometimes mandated by some applications. For example, when a message publisher comes back after a crash, the replay of the messages should appear in an orderly fashion.

The Resequencer component has the ability to order the incoming messages. For example, if 10 messages are published to a channel but in the wrong order, the consumer plugged in *after* the Resequencer does its work will receive all of them in a predefined sequence, e.g., message 1, message 2, etc.

The Resequencers work on the `SEQUENCE_NUMBER` header field to track the sequences. Say a message numbered 8 (out of 10 child messages) is the first to arrive; the Resequencer does not publish this message, since message number 1 (the first `SEQUENCE_NUMBER`) or messages numbered 2 through 7 have not arrived. Message 8 (along with any other out-of-order messages) is hence stored either in-memory or in the database until the entire set has arrived and is reordered. The exception is if you set a `release-partial-sequences` flag to `true`, which would publish the sequences as soon as they are gathered, rather than waiting for the whole group.

The `resequencer` element in the integration namespace is used to define a Resequencer as shown in the following snippet:

```
<int:resequencer input-channel="all-in-reseq-channel"
                 output-channel="reseq-channel"
                 release-partial-sequences="true">
</int:resequencer>
```

Summary

The messaging flow components are critical to design any business flow. This chapter discussed such components in detail. The Filters are the endpoints that allow or disallow messages based on a set of predefined criteria. Routers mainly distribute the messages based on a routing algorithm. The rest of the chapter described another set of flow components consisting of Splitters, Aggregators, and Resequencers. Splitters mainly slice the message stream into smaller pieces, while the Aggregators reassemble them back into the original message. The Resequencer waits for a set of messages to arrive and, if necessary, reorders them before they are reassembled.

CHAPTER 7

Adapters

Introduction

Using messaging as a medium to integrate with external systems can often be a challenging task. There are various issues to consider, including the complexity of connection mechanisms and the transformation of the message formats produced by different systems. In addition, organizations usually have disparate system interactions, e.g., booking trades against external brokers, fetching data files from an intra-site file systems, consuming messages from an external JMS, or posting a company CEO's feed to Twitter. You will need to write integration adapters, either developing them in-house or buying them off the shelf.

As these are common organizational requirements, the ideal solution would be an open-source framework that can be extended or configured according to the needs of an individual or an organization. Spring Integration is this ideal framework that provides many adapters out of the box.

All adapters are very similar—working as inbound and outbound adapters. Inbound adapters fetch files or database resultsets. Outbound adapters do the opposite, taking the messages off the channels and converting them to files, then transferring them onto a file system or database record to persist them to the database.

The fundamentals are explained in the first section—File Adapters. The other adapters work in similar ways, except for differences related to underlying resources where the artifacts are picked up or published to.

File Adapters

File Adapters fetch or copy files to and from different file systems. They pick a file from a file system and turn into Framework's `Message` to publish onto a channel and vice versa. Framework supports a declarative model using `file` namespace. It also provides a few classes for reading and writing files, but using namespace is advised.

Using Namespace

The file namespace provides the respective elements to create the objects declaratively and easily. In order to use the file namespace, you should add the respective schema urls to your XML file, highlighted in bold below:

```
<?xml version="1.0" encoding="UTF-8"?>
 <beans
    ....
    xmlns:file="http://www.springframework.org/schema/integration/file"
  xsi:schemaLocation=
    http://www.springframework.org/schema/integration/file
    http://www.springframework.org/schema/integration/file/spring-integration-
    file-2.1.xsd">
    ...
 </beans>
```

Framework provides two adapters to read and write the files. The inbound-channel-adapter element is used for reading the files and publishing them onto a channel as File payload messages. The outbound-channel-adapter is used for picking up the File payload messages from a channel, extracting them as files, and writing them to the file systems.

Inbound File Adapter

The following snippet demonstrates the inbound adapter:

```
<!-- Adapter using namespace -->
<file:inbound-channel-adapter id="fileAdapter"
  directory="/Users/mkonda/dev/ws/" channel="files-out-channel">

  <int:poller fixed-rate="1000" />
</file:inbound-channel-adapter>
```

The endpoint picks up the files from the given directory and publishes them as Message<File> messages onto a files-out-channel indicated by the channel attribute. The poller will indicate the rate at which the files should be polled (one second in the above example).

For simplicity's sake, wire in a stdout-channel-adapter that will pick up the messages from files-out-channel and print them to the console:

```
<int-stream:stdout-channel-adapter
  id="files-out-channel" />
```

File Adapter Settings

There are some settings that the file adapters can take.

Preventing Duplicate Files. A file reader should have the flexibility to pick up a predefined set of files instead of reading all of them from the directory. This requirement is satisfied by the filters that we set in the adapters. The prevent-duplicates is a simple tag that lets the reader fetch only files that were not picked up in the earlier runs. Note that this

will only be true per session, as the reader does not hold state. If the reader restarts, it
will redeliver the same files.

```
<file:inbound-channel-adapter id="fileAdapter"
  directory="/Users/mkonda/dev/ws/"
  channel="files-out-channel"
  prevent-duplicates="true">

  <int:poller fixed-rate="1000" />
</file:inbound-channel-adapter>
```

Filters. Filtering is done by using an implementation of the `FileListFilter` interface.
Framework has a class named `AcceptOnceFileListFilter` which accepts the file only
once in the current session and thus prevents duplicate fetching.

If you need to customize the filtering further, you must implement `FileListFilter`:

```
public class PositionsFilter implements FileListFilter<Position> {
  public List<Position> filterFiles(Position[] files) {
    List<Position> filteredList = new ArrayList<Position>();
    // implement your filtering logic here
    return filteredList;
  }
}
```

In addition to preventing duplicates, you can set up filters using the `filename-pattern` and `filename-regex` attributes.

```
<file:inbound-channel-adapter id="positionsAdapter"
  ...
  filename-pattern="*.pos">
  ...
</file:inbound-channel-adapter>
```

The above adapter fetches only files that have the pos extension. If you wish to fetch
the files based on a regular expression, use the `filename-regex` attribute as shown
below:

```
<file:inbound-channel-adapter id="positionsAdapter"
  directory="/Users/mkonda/dev/ws/"
  ...
  filename-regex="[ABC]_positions.pos">
</file:inbound-channel-adapter>
```

The adapter fetches only files that start with A, B, or C and have a pos extension. Other
files will be ignored.

File Locks. You can also lock files so that other processes will not read the same file as
you. You can use Framework's `FileLocker` implementation with the `nio-locker`
attribute:

```
<file:inbound-channel-adapter id="positionsAdapter"
  directory="/Users/mkonda/dev/ws/" channel="positions-files-channel"
  prevent-duplicates="true" filename-regex="[ABC]_positions.pos">

  <file:nio-locker/>
```

```
    <int:poller fixed-rate="1000" />
  </file:inbound-channel-adapter>
```

You can also throw in your own customized locker:

```
<file:inbound-channel-adapter id="positionsAdapter"
  directory="/Users/mkonda/dev/ws/" channel="positions-files-channel"
  prevent-duplicates="true" filename-regex="[ABC]_positions.pos">
  <!-- use custom locker -->
  <file:locker ref="positionsLocker"/>
  <int:poller fixed-rate="1000" />
</file:inbound-channel-adapter>

<bean id="positionsLocker"
  class="com.madhusudhan.jsi.adapters.PositionsFileLocker"/>
```

The positionsLocker refers to the custom class PositionsFileLocker that implements the FileLocker interface.

Standalone File Readers

If you have chosen not to use the declarative model, then you may choose to use Framework's classes. The file reader is represented by the FileReadingMessageSource class. It implements Framework's MessageSource interface with one method: receive(). This is a base interface implemented by all the sources that require polling for messages. The return value is a Message object with java.io.File as a payload.

The FileReadingMessageSource can be used as a simple bean to read the files as messages. The StandaloneFileAdapterTest below shows such a case. All you have to do is to instantiate the class and set a few properties, such as the directory in which you can find the files.

```
public class StandaloneFileAdapterTest {
  // set the directory from where the files need to be picked up
  File directory = new File("/Users/mkonda/dev/ws");

  public void startStandaloneAdatper() {
    FileReadingMessageSource src = new FileReadingMessageSource();
    src.setDirectory(directory);
    Message<File> msg = src.receive();
    System.out.println("Received:"+msg);
  }

  public static void main(String[] args) {
    StandaloneFileAdapterTest test = new StandaloneFileAdapterTest();
    test.startAdatper();
  }
}
```

The receive method produces a Message with the File as a payload. You can also create the class as a bean declaratively in an XML file instead of coupling the bean in your source code. We have declared the FileReadingMessageSource in the following file:

```
// declaring the framework's class as a bean
<bean id="positionsReader"
  class="org.springframework.integration.file.FileReadingMessageSource">
  <property name="directory" value="/Users/mkonda/dev/ws/" />
</bean>
```

Execute the application so the context loads the bean by reading the above XML file. Use the context API to get the bean instance and invoke the receive method. This is shown below:

```
private void startAdapterUsingDeclaredBeanRef() {
  ctx = new ClassPathXmlApplicationContext(
    "adapters-file-beans.xml");
  fileReader = ctx.getBean("fileReader", FileReadingMessageSource.class);

  // now you got the instance, poll for msgs
  Message<File> msg = fileReader.receive();
  System.out.println("Message received from the bean:" + msg);
}
```

The missing piece is to create a publisher so that all of the file messages are published onto a channel. This is not done by FileReadingMessageSource and we need to look for an alternative to create a standard publisher.

Outbound Adapters

The fileWriter adapter's job is to consume messages from a channel and write them to a file system. The framework provides classes that you can instantiate as normal Java Objects or write as beans in your XML config file. Alternatively, you can use the outbound-channel-adapter element in file namespace for declaring the adapter entirely in an XML config file.

You can use namespace's outbound-channel-adapter element to set up an outbound file adapter:

```
<file:outbound-channel-adapter
  directory="/Users/mkonda/dev/ws/tmp"
  channel="positions-file-channel"/>
```

The adapter receives the messages from the positions-file-channel and writes them to the filesystem directory defined by the directory attribute.

The following setup creates an inbound adapter which fetches the files from a predefined directory and publishes them onto an output channel. The outbound adapter then consumes these messages from the same channel and writes them to a different directory. The whole execution just requires the following lines in the XML file:

```
<file:inbound-channel-adapter id="inAdapter"
  directory="/Users/mkonda/dev/ws/"
  channel="file-channel">
  <int:poller fixed-rate="1000"/>
</file:inbound-channel-adapter>
```

```
<file:outbound-channel-adapter id="outAdapter"
  channel="file-channel"
  directory="/Users/mkonda/dev/ws/tmp"/>
```

Standalone File Adapters

Using `standalone` class is straightforward: instantiate the `FileWritingMessageHandler` with a directory location where the files will be written. The code snippet is shown below:

```
// set the directory
File directory = new File("/Users/mkonda/dev/ws/tmp");
..
private void startStandaloneWriter() {

  // fetch the channel for incoming feed
  outChannel = ctx.getBean("files-channel",
    PublishSubscribeChannel.class);

  handler = new FileWritingMessageHandler(directory);
  // subscribe to the incoming feed
  outChannel.subscribe(handler);
}
```

You have to submit this handler to the channel so messages will be passed onto this event handler.

FTP Adapters

Remote files are usually fetched by employing the File Transfer Protocol (FTP), while local files are transferred onto a remote server using the same FTP. These two tasks are supported by the framework using inbound and outbound channel adapters.

The inbound channel adapters connect to an FTP Server to fetch the remote files and pass them as messages with the current file (`Message<File>`) as payload. The outbound channel adapters act in the opposite direction: they connect to channels, consume the messages, and write them to remote server directories.

Both adapters, represented by `inbound-channel-adapter` and `outbound-channel-adapter`, are included in the `ftp` namespace support. Before setting up the adapters, one critical piece of information is required by the adapters: connection (or session) details.

Session Factory

The adapters should know the server details to connect to, including the username and password. Framework's `DefaultFtpSessionConnectionFactory` class provides these details. You should declare this bean in your `config` file with the appropriate properties set. The bean reference is then provided to the adapters as a `session-factory` attribute.

First, let's see how we can set up a session factory. In your XML file, declare the factory class and provide the necessary details:

```
<bean name="sessionFactory"
  class="org.springframework.integration.ftp.session.DefaultFtpSessionFactory">
  <property name="host" value="ftp.madhusudhan.com"/>
  <property name="username" value="jsi"/>
  <property name="password" value="******"/>
  ...
</bean>
```

Once you have the connection factory declared, the next step is to wire the factory to the adapters. Note that you can read the properties from a file instead of hard-coding them using the Property placeholders.

Inbound FTP Adapters

Inbound FTP Adapters connect to a remote server using the connection factory and poll for files on the remote file system. If a file is found, it will be consumed by the component and a message with `File` as the payload (`Message<File>`) will be created. This message is then sent to the channel to be collected further processing.

First, you have to add the necessary schema definitions to your XML file:

```
<?xml version="1.0" encoding="UTF-8"?>
<beans
  ....
  xmlns:ftp="http://www.springframework.org/schema/integration/ftp"
xsi:schemaLocation=
  "http://www.springframework.org/schema/integration/ftp
    http://www.springframework.org/schema/integration/ftp/spring-integration-
ftp-2.1.xsd
  ....">
</beans>
```

The `inbound-channel-adapter` in the `ftp` namespace is used to configure the adapter:

```
<ftp:inbound-channel-adapter channel="positions-channel"
  session-factory="sessionFactory"
  remote-directory="/feeds/systems/positions/"
  local-directory="/feeds/in/positions/">

  <int:poller fixed-rate="1000"/>
</ftp:inbound-channel-adapter>

<bean name="sessionFactory"
  class="org.springframework.integration.ftp.session.DefaultFtpSessionFactory">
  ...
</bean>
```

The component will use the session factory to connect to the remote server, pick up files from the `remote-directory`, and publish them to the channel. You can set properties such as `filename-pattern`, `filename-regex`, and others according to the application's need.

The presence of `local-directory` in the adapter config might have raised a question in your mind. When the adapter starts polling, before it even gets the remote files, it looks for the files under `local-directory` and publishes those files as Messages. Once all the local files are published, then the remote files are polled and transferred.

You can also use your own filter classes by setting the bean on the filter attribute, e.g. `filter="myPositionsFtpFilter"`. The filtering was discussed in the *File Adapters* section and the same principle also applies to FTP adapters.

Outbound FTP Adapters

The `outbound-channel-adapter` element is used to create an endpoint for publishing the messages onto a remote file system using the FTP:

```
<ftp:outbound-channel-adapter channel="positions-channel"
  remote-directory="/feeds/systems/positions/"
  session-factory="connectionFactory">

  <int:poller fixed-rate="1000" />
</ftp:outbound-channel-adapter>
```

It requires a session factory that holds the server details. The messages are consumed from `positions-channel` and written to the `/feeds/systems/positions` remote directory.

Caching Sessions

The framework creates a pool of FTP sessions on both the inbound and outbound channel adapters to optimize the network calls. You can tweak the `cache-sessions` by setting it to `false` so that the sessions are not cached and pooled. By default, this setting is true, that is, the sessions are always cached.

```
<ftp:outbound-channel-adapter channel="positions-channel"
  cache-sessions="false"
  ...
</ftp:outbound-channel-adapter>
```

JMS Adapters

The Spring Integration framework provides good support for integrating Spring applications with Java Messaging Service (JMS).

If you are new to JMS, I would recommend reading my *Just Spring* book that explains the concepts of JMS at a high level.

The framework provides inbound and outbound adapters for receiving and sending messages across to external messaging systems. The inbound adapters will pick up a message from a JMS destination (`topic` or `queue`) and publish them onto local channels. On the other hand, the outbound adapters will convert a local payload from a channel into JMS Message and publish to a JMS destination (`topic` or `queue`).

The jms namespace defines the relevant elements to use these adapters declaratively.

Inbound Adapters: Receiving Messages

Receiving messages from a messaging system may involve some complexity. This is due to the fact that the consumption might be driven by the consumer client or by the provider. In the former case, the client will have to poll for messages on a regular basis, while the latter case ensures that the client is given a message when it arrives on a server (hence message-driven or event-driven).

Synchronous Consumers

As explained, the `inbound-channel-adapter` is responsible for receiving messages from a JMS Server. The endpoint is configured to connect to a JMS Server, fetch the messages, and publish them onto a local channel. Note that this is a polling consumer. In the backend, it uses the `JmsTemplate's receive` method to poll for messages. You can either provide an instance of `JmsTemplate` or provide `connectionFactory` and `destination` together.

Here are the basic settings for the inbound adapter:

```xml
<jms:inbound-channel-adapter id="positionsJmsAdapter"
  connection-factory="connectionFactory"
  destination="positionsQueue"
  channel="positions-channel">
  <int:poller fixed-rate="1000" />
</jms:inbound-channel-adapter>

<!-- destination on ActiveMQ -->
<bean id="positionsQueue" class="org.apache.activemq.command.ActiveMQQueue">
  <constructor-arg value="POSITIONS_QUEUE" />
</bean>

<!-- connection factory for ActiveMQ -->
<bean name="connectionFactory" class="org.apache.activemq.ActiveMQConnectionFactory">
  <property name="brokerURL">
    <value>tcp://localhost:61616</value>
  </property>
</bean>
```

The connection factory encapsulates the details required to connect to an external JMS Provider. This is defined simply as a bean and wired into the adapter using a `connection-factory` attribute. If the name of the bean is already `connectionFactory`, you don't have to declare this attribute because the adapter defaults to wire a bean named `connectionFactory`. I am using ActiveMQ as the provider and hence the `brokerURL` points to my local ActiveMQ server.

The second thing to note is the destination. This is a JMS `Destination` object which is basically a `Queue` in terms of JMS terminology. The adapter connects to the `localhost`

ActiveMQ server, checks the POSITIONS_QUEUE, fetches any messages it finds, and publishes to the local application's channel, positions-channel.

Message-Driven Consumers

The second type of consumer is driven by the server based on subscriptions to the channels. The message-driven-channel-adapter element represents this type of consumer. The consumer expects an instance of a Spring MessageListener container or a combination of connectionFactory and destination. The following snippet shows the basic settings:

```
<!-- Event Driven consumer-->
<jms:message-driven-channel-adapter id="msgDrivenPositionsAdapter"
  connection-factory="connectionFactory"
  destination="positionsQueue"
  channel="positions-channel">
</jms:message-driven-channel-adapter>
```

The connection factory and destination beans remain the same. However, we have not provided a poller because it is an event-based consumer.

There's a bit of conversion required to transform a Spring's object to JMS Message type and vice versa. The extract-payload attribute is used to transform the payloads, discussed in the next section.

Payload Conversions

When the message is published onto our local channels, what is the type of that payload? How is it constructed? This depends on the converters being used. We use converters to extract the body of a JMS Message and set it as payload onto a local (non-JMS) message. The default converter used by the framework is SimpleMessageConverter, which converts the body to its respective payload. If the JMS Message is a TextMessage, the body is wrapped as String message, and if it's a ByteMessage, it is converted to bytes, etc.

One more thing to note: the conversion begins only when the attribute extract-payload is set to true. By default, it is set to true (so conversions do happen automatically if you don't provide this flag). However, if you switch off this flag, then the JMS Message is sent along with the payload.

You can provide a custom converter by adding a tag called message-converter, which points to your customized bean:

```
<jms:message-driven-channel-adapter
  id="msgDrivenPositionsAdapter"
  ...
  message-converter="positionsConverter">
</jms:message-driven-channel-adapter>
<bean id="positionsConverter"
  class="com.madhusudhan.jsi.adapters.jms.PositionsConverter">
```

Publishing Messages: Outbound Adapters

The outbound adapter's duty is to fetch messages from the channel and publish them to JMS `Queue` or `Topic`. The `outbound-channel-adapter` element is used to create an endpoint that will perform this activity:

```
<jms:outbound-channel-adapter channel="positions-channel"
  connection-factory="connectionFactory"
  destination="positionsQueue">
  <int:poller fixed-rate="1000"/>
</jms:outbound-channel-adapter>
```

The underlying class being used for this function is `JmsSendingMessageHandler`. In the above snippet, you can see how the channel messages are taken by the adapter and published onto `positionsQueue`, which is a JMS `Queue`.

The `extract-payload` is the reverse. When set to `true`, the adapter will convert the channel's payload as equivalent to a JMS `Message` body. For example, a `String` payload is extracted as `TextMessage`, and so on.

JDBC Adapters

Following the same scheme of inbound and outbound adapters, the framework's JDBC adapters don't do anything different. The inbound adapter extracts the data from `Database` and passes the resultset as a `Message` onto the local channels. The outbound adapter persists the data records into `Database` by reading off the channel. The `jdbc` name-support provides the relevant elements for creating the respective adapters.

It would be ideal if you were familiar with JDBC and especially Spring Framework's support. JDBC discusses things about `JdbcTemplate`, Row Mapping strategies, etc., which will be useful for understanding the adapters outlined below.

You can read my other book, Just Spring (*http://oreil.ly/just-spring*), for a basic primer on these concepts.

Inbound JDBC Adapters

It is the responsibility of inbound adapters to read a data set and convert them to messages. The `inbound-channel-adapter` is used to create an endpoint of this sort. The adapter is provided with a SQL query and a channel to post the messages. It is also given an instance of `Datasource`, which will provide the relevant database connection details. You can also provide the `JdbcTemplate`.

See the basic setup here:

```
<jdbc:inbound-channel-adapter channel="resultset-channel"
  data-source="mySqlDatasource"
  query="SELECT * FROM ACCOUNTS A
    where A.STATUS='NEW' and POLLED='N'">
```

```
    <int:poller fixed-rate="1000"/>
  </jdbc:inbound-channel-adapter>
```

The above adapter connects to the Database identified by the data source. It then uses the query attribute to execute the query and fetches the results that match the criteria. Currently it is running a query on the ACCOUNTS table to fetch only non-polled records and accounts whose status is NEW. These records are then transformed into Framework's Message and published onto resultset-channel.

The whole result set is converted into a single message with a payload of List records. The type of the records depends on your row mapping strategy.

In the above configuration, you can see that we have provided a poller which sends the adapter to the database every one second to fetch the records.

Sometimes, we may not wish to include the same list of records extracted from one poll in the next poll. In order to exclude the already polled records, Framework provides an update statement to be attached to the poll. That is, every time we poll, we update the record with the setting specified in the select query so the select query will not fetch those updated records.

For example, we only wish to query with newly created Account records. So, what we can do is update a column (of course, it should be part of the table) called POLLED.

```
<jdbc:inbound-channel-adapter channel="resultset-channel"
  data-source="mySqlDatasource"
  query="SELECT * FROM ACCOUNTS A where A.STATUS='NEW' and POLLED='N'"
  update="UPDATE ACCONTS set POLLED='Y' where ACCOUNT_ID in (:ACCOUNT_ID)">
  <int:poller fixed-rate="1000" />
</jdbc:inbound-channel-adapter>
```

The convention followed in the update is that the values that the select query finds are passed as parameters to the update statement using a colon (:).

Outbound JDBC Adapters

The outbound JDBC adapters are used to execute SQL queries in the database. The SQL query is constructed with the appropriate value fetched from the incoming Message. So, the outbound adapter listens on a message channel, picks up a message, extracts the relevant values, constructs the query and executes the query on the Database.

Let's look at an example where every Trade message appearing on a trade-persistence-channel should be persisted. Under normal circumstances, we could have written a consumer that picks up each message and then uses persistence mechanics to store the message in the database. However, Spring Integration's outbound adapter saves you from writing this extra code.

All we have to do is configure an outbound adapter with the relevant details. The following snippet demonstrates this:

```
<jdbc:outbound-channel-adapter
  channel="trades-persistence-channel"
  data-source="mySqlDatasource"
  query="insert into TRADE t(ID,ACCOUNT,INSTRUMENT)
    values(:payload[TRADE_ID], :payload[TRADE_ACCOUNT],
    :payload[TRADE_INSTRUMENT])">
</jdbc:outbound-channel-adapter>
```

The interesting point from the above snippet is the query. The query can be formulated using the payload key tags. That is, the incoming message will have a payload of Map type from which the map is queried using ID, ACCOUNT, etc. You can also use header's Map values:

```
qyery="insert into TRADE t(ID,ACCOUNT,INSTRUMENT,EXPIRY)
    values(:payload[TRADE_ID], :payload[TRADE_ACCOUNT],
    :payload[TRADE_INSTRUMENT], :headers[EXPIRY])">
```

The Map message is created as shown below:

```
public Message<Map<String, Object>> createTradeMessage(){
  Map<String, Object> tradeMap = new HashMap<String, Object>();
  tradeMap.put("ID", "1929303d");
  tradeMap.put("ACCOUNT", "ACC12345");
  //..
  // Create a Msg using MessageBuilder
  Message<Map<String, Object>> tradeMsg =
    MessageBuilder.withPayload(tradeMap).build();

  return tradeMsg;
}
```

Once this message is sent to the persistence-channel, it will be consumed by the adapter and the query automatically executed on the Database.

Summary

This chapter laid out the foundations on the fundamentals of integration adapters. It discussed major adapters such as File, FTP, JDBC, and JMS adapters. We have seen a common characteristic across the adapters—inbound adapters will get the data from the sources and publish them onto the local channels, while outbound adapters read the messages off the channels and push them onto the source systems.

About the Author

Madhusudhan Konda is an experienced Java consultant working in London, primarily with investment banks and financial organizations. Having worked in Enterprise and core Java for the last 12 years, his interests lie in distributed, multi-threaded, n-tier scalable, and extensible architectures. He is experienced in designing and developing high-frequency and low-latency application architectures. He enjoys writing technical papers and is interested in mentoring.

Get even more for your money.

Join the O'Reilly Community, and register the O'Reilly books you own. It's free, and you'll get:

- $4.99 ebook upgrade offer
- 40% upgrade offer on O'Reilly print books
- Membership discounts on books and events
- Free lifetime updates to ebooks and videos
- Multiple ebook formats, DRM FREE
- Participation in the O'Reilly community
- Newsletters
- Account management
- 100% Satisfaction Guarantee

Signing up is easy:

1. **Go to: oreilly.com/go/register**
2. **Create an O'Reilly login.**
3. **Provide your address.**
4. **Register your books.**

Note: English-language books only

To order books online:
oreilly.com/store

For questions about products or an order:
orders@oreilly.com

To sign up to get topic-specific email announcements and/or news about upcoming books, conferences, special offers, and new technologies:
elists@oreilly.com

For technical questions about book content:
booktech@oreilly.com

To submit new book proposals to our editors:
proposals@oreilly.com

O'Reilly books are available in multiple DRM-free ebook formats. For more information:
oreilly.com/ebooks

O'REILLY®

Spreading the knowledge of innovators   oreilly.com

Have it your way.

O'Reilly eBooks

- Lifetime access to the book when you buy through oreilly.com
- Provided in up to four DRM-free file formats, for use on the devices of your choice: PDF, .epub, Kindle-compatible .mobi, and Android .apk
- Fully searchable, with copy-and-paste and print functionality
- Alerts when files are updated with corrections and additions

oreilly.com/ebooks/

Safari Books Online

- Access the contents and quickly search over 7000 books on technology, business, and certification guides
- Learn from expert video tutorials, and explore thousands of hours of video on technology and design topics
- Download whole books or chapters in PDF format, at no extra cost, to print or read on the go
- Get early access to books as they're being written
- Interact directly with authors of upcoming books
- Save up to 35% on O'Reilly print books

See the complete Safari Library at safari.oreilly.com

O'REILLY®

Spreading the knowledge of innovators.   oreilly.com

Lightning Source UK Ltd.
Milton Keynes UK
UKHW031821270120
357693UK00008B/401